Cloning

Other books in the Great Medical Discoveries series:

Gene Therapy
Tuberculosis
Vaccines

Great Medical Discoveries

Cloning

by Don Nardo

Library of Congress Cataloging-in-Publication Data

Nardo, Don, 1947–
  Cloning / by Don Nardo.
    p. cm. — (Great medical discoveries)
Includes bibliographical references and index.
  ISBN 1-56006-927-9 (hbk. : alk. paper)
  1. Cloning—Juvenile literature. [1. Cloning.] I. Title. II.
Series.
  QH442.2 .N37 2002
  660.6'5—dc21

2001002556

Copyright © 2002 by Lucent Books, Inc.
P.O. Box 289011, San Diego, CA 92198-9011
Printed in the U.S.A.

CONTENTS

FOREWORD

Throughout history, people have struggled to understand and conquer the diseases and physical ailments that plague us. Once in a while, a discovery has changed the course of medicine and sometimes, the course of history itself. The stories of these discoveries have many elements in common—accidental findings, sudden insights, human dedication, and most of all, powerful results. Many illnesses that in the past were essentially a death warrant for their sufferers are today curable or even virtually extinct. And exciting new directions in medicine promise a future in which the building blocks of human life itself—the genes—may be manipulated and altered to restore health or to prevent disease from occurring in the first place.

It has been said that an insight is simply a rearrangement of already-known facts, and as often as not, these great medical discoveries have resulted partly from a reexamination of earlier efforts in light of new knowledge. Nineteenth-century monk Gregor Mendel experimented with pea plants for years, quietly unlocking the mysteries of genetics. However, the importance of his findings went unnoticed until three separate scientists, studying cell division with a newly improved invention called a microscope, rediscovered his work decades after his death. French doctor Jean-Antoine Villemin's experiments with rabbits proved that tuberculosis was contagious, but his conclusions were politely ignored by the medical community until another doctor, Robert Koch of Germany, discovered the exact culprit—the tubercle bacillus germ—years later.

Accident, too, has played a part in some medical discoveries. Because the tuberculosis germ does not stain with dye as easily as other bacteria, Koch was able to see it only after he had let a treated slide sit far longer than he intended. An unwanted speck of mold led Englishman Alexander Fleming to recognize the bacteria-killing qualities of the penicillium fungi, ushering in the era of antibiotic "miracle drugs."

That researchers sometimes benefited from fortuitous accidents does not mean that they were bumbling amateurs who relied solely on luck. They were dedicated scientists whose work created the conditions under which such lucky events could occur; many sacrificed years of their lives to observation and experimentation. Sometimes the price they paid was higher. Rene Launnec, who invented the stethoscope to help him study the effects of tuberculosis, himself succumbed to the disease.

And humanity has benefited from these scientists' efforts. The formerly terrifying disease of smallpox has been eliminated from the face of the earth—the only case of the complete conquest of a once deadly disease. Tuberculosis, perhaps the oldest disease known to humans and certainly one of its most prolific killers, has been essentially wiped out in some parts of the world. Genetically engineered insulin is a godsend to countless diabetics who are allergic to the animal insulin that has traditionally been used to help them.

Despite such triumphs there are few unequivocal success stories in the history of great medical discoveries. New strains of tuberculosis are proving to be resistant to the antibiotics originally developed to treat them, raising the specter of a resurgence of the disease that has killed 2 billion people over the course of human history. But medical research continues on numerous fronts and will no doubt lead to still undreamed-of advancements in the future.

Each volume in the Great Medical Discoveries series tells the story of one great medical breakthrough—the first gropings for understanding, the pieces that came together and how, and the immediate and longer-term results. Part science and part social history, the series explains some of the key findings that have shaped modern medicine and relieved untold human suffering. Numerous primary and secondary source quotations enhance the text and bring to life all the drama of scientific discovery. Sidebars highlight personalities and convey personal stories. The series also discusses the future of each medical discovery—a future in which vaccines may guard against AIDS, gene therapy may eliminate cancer, and other as-yet unimagined treatments may become commonplace.

INTRODUCTION

Cloning: An Increasingly Divisive Issue

Cloning is presently one of the most controversial and hotly debated science-related issues across the developed world. Early in 2001, many newspapers, magazines, radio programs, and television news and talk shows began devoting increased coverage to cloning. More often than not, at least one of the interviewees or other participants was a member of a major religious organization who expressed concerns about the moral and ethical implications of cloning. Responding to such concerns by numerous ordinary citizens as well as religious leaders, a committee of the U.S. House of Representatives met in March 2001 to examine several unresolved issues relating to cloning research in the United States. Meanwhile, several countries, including Japan, Germany, Denmark, Australia, and the United Kingdom had already banned certain kinds of cloning research, reflecting widespread fears and concerns among the citizens of those nations. "To many if not most of us," say Martha Nussbaum and Cass Sunstein, authors of the recent book, *Clones and Clones*,

> cloning represents a possible turning point in the history of humanity. Some view the prospect with alarm; some with disgust; some with joy; some with grief for the life we

Pope John Paul II (seated, right) is one of many religious leaders who condemns the idea of cloning human embryos.

used to have, and will shortly have no longer. Some, too, are calm and matter-of-fact about the entire affair, urging us to let science take its course before we conclude that dreadful things are at hand. But almost everyone is asking questions.[1]

What exactly is cloning, and what is all the fuss about it? Cloning involves genes, the tiny particles in the cells of all living things that carry the blueprints for reproduction. Characteristics such as eye and hair color, body type, and susceptibility to certain conditions and diseases are most commonly transmitted genetically through sexual relations between two individuals, male and female, of a species. In the case of a clone, however, only one parent is involved. The parent can be either male *or* female. As science writer David Jefferis explains:

A clone is a living thing that has exactly the same genes as its parent. In sexual reproduction, genes from both male and female parents are mixed to create children that have genes from both their father and mother. A clone has the genes of only one parent, so it is identical to the parent.[2]

Some cloning goes on naturally among certain kinds of plants and a few types of primitive, very simple animals. Humans early on learned to clone plants to produce healthier, more plentiful, and more useful varieties. And in the twentieth century, a few scientists began experimenting with animal cloning. That research culminated in the creation of the clone of a sheep, named Dolly, by Scottish scientists in 1996. Animal cloning technology holds promise for a host of benefits, including breeding stronger, more productive and cost-efficient herds of cattle, growing animal organs for transplanting into humans, and saving endangered species.

Dolly the sheep, the first higher animal to be successfully cloned from an adult animal.

Questions That Have Never Been Asked

It is not plant or animal cloning alone that fuels the present concerns, fears, and widespread debate on the subject, however. Rather, the controversy stems largely from widely publicized announcements made by scientists working in two separate, well-funded labs that they are purposely and actively engaged in an attempt to clone human beings. One of these labs is located in Canada, the other in a secret location; and literally hundreds of similar labs across the globe are presently cloning animals and conducting genetic research that improves the techniques needed to clone humans. Does that mean that human cloning is definitely just around the corner? Virtually all biologists and geneticists are now convinced that it is. About the Canadian group, Gregory Stock, director of the UCLA Program on Medicine, Technology, and Society, says, "They certainly have what's necessary to make a solid attempt [to clone a human]. And in any case," he adds, "what they are doing is of symbolic significance. If they don't succeed, someone else will in the next five years."[3]

The seeming certainty that human cloning will soon be not only a reality, but also increasingly common, raises numerous questions that no one has considered before. For example, might the ability to make genetic copies of people allow unscrupulous individuals or groups to exploit these copies in nefarious ways (perhaps by manufacturing armies of henchmen or growing mindless bodies in tanks to harvest their organs for a profit)? Or on a more basic level, would the person who provided the cell to create a clone be that clone's biological parent or merely his or her identical twin, though a generation removed? Would clones be as socially accepted as other people? Or would they suffer from some kind of stigma that might harm them psychologically? Or might clones be subjected to unreasonable expectations or demands to act—and even think—like their cell donors? Will clones show higher rates of cancer or other diseases than people created the traditional

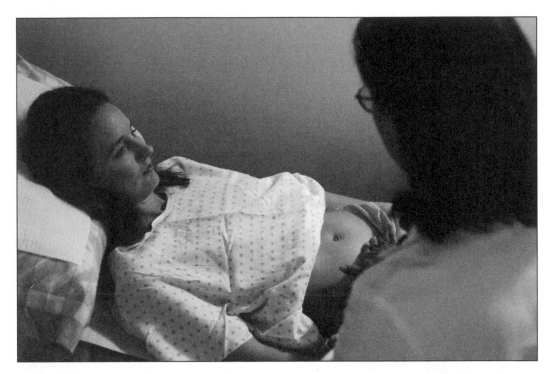

way? Because human cloning will be, at least for the foreseeable future, a very expensive endeavor, will the majority of people cloned be wealthy individuals and their kin? And might that fact not lead to new kinds of class hatred? An even more profound and far-reaching question is whether people will eventually stop having babies through sexual means in favor of the cloning process; this could conceivably take away the age-old element of chance in the reproductive process and allow parents to design healthy children with whatever traits and abilities they might choose.

A pregnant woman visits her doctor. Some people wonder whether the natural way of getting pregnant— sexual reproduction— might some day become less common in favor of cloning.

Miracle or Menace?

For some people, these and the many other questions and potentialities emerging from cloning research are disquieting, even frightening. Many suggest that cloning humans may be unethical, or against God's will, or that the process should be banned or at the very least strictly regulated. Others, by contrast, see grappling with the social and ethical questions about cloning as fascinating or challenging, or they simply accept it as an inevitable part of the emergence of a powerful new technology. Moreover, they point out the possible benefits of cloning humans, such as providing infertile couples with another way to have a baby using their own genetic material.

Still other people find themselves in the middle on the issue. Feeling that they presently lack sufficient knowledge about cloning and its social and moral implications, they can see possible positive as well as negative aspects. As Nancy Duff, of the Princeton Theological Seminary, puts it, "Many people wonder if this is a miracle for which we can thank God, or an ominous new way to play God ourselves."[4]

Many unknowns exist about cloning technology and where it might lead. But one thing is certain: The future scientific, social, and legal implications of cloning are presently wide open to interpretation by individuals,

Until now, abortion has been one of the most contentious medical-social issues; cloning may become an even more hotly debated issue.

courts, and governments. So the issue is bound to get even more controversial and divisive in the near future as people with contrasting views about cloning take and defend their respective sides. "In the coming years," warns one informed observer, "the angry standoffs on abortion between Pro-Life and Pro-Choice groups may seem mild compared to the polarization of society over human cloning."[5]

CHAPTER 1

Before Dolly: Cloning in Nature, Agriculture, and the Imagination

Long before Dolly the sheep made headlines, before human farmers began cloning crops, and in fact before humans beings even evolved, clones existed. Indeed, nature has been cloning plants and animals on its own for hundreds of millions of years. Bacteria and other kinds of one-celled creatures reproduce by cloning, as do certain kinds of multicelled plants and animals. When humans arrived on the scene, they invented agriculture. And eventually they found that they could imitate nature by artificially cloning certain kinds of fruits and vegetables. By selecting the biggest, tastiest, most disease-resistant variety of a certain fruit and cloning it, for example, they could ensure more productive and valuable harvests of that fruit.

In the twentieth century, growing food by artificial cloning became a big business. Some scientists naturally assumed that finding a way to clone domestic animals, such as cattle, sheep, and pigs, would be a similar boon, since it would produce bigger, healthier, more valuable herds. However, cloning animals proved to be tremendously more difficult than cloning plants. Even attempts to clone frogs, which are much less sophisticated animals than mammals, failed. And throughout most of the century, many scientists considered the possibility of cloning domestic livestock, much less humans, an elusive, if not impossible goal.

Meanwhile, public attitudes toward the idea of cloning were mostly shaped and conditioned by the popular media. Animal cloning and especially human cloning became increasingly frequent subjects of science fiction writers and filmmakers, who in the second half of the twentieth century developed and expressed a fascination for stories about the dangers of science run amok. Cloning joined artificial life (the Frankenstein factor), robots, atomic energy, genetic engineering, and artificial intelligence as possible means for demented or evil individuals to unleash havoc on the world. The perception developed in the public imagination that if human cloning were indeed possible, it was bound to be used in ominous, immoral, or dangerous ways.

The 1996 film Multiplicity, *starring Michael Keaton, is just one movie in which filmmakers have dealt with the cloning concept.*

Nature's Abundant Clones

This widespread negative perception of the future possibilities of animal and human cloning was based to some degree on ignorance of what cloning really is. Thanks to the sensational depictions in books and movies, to the average person the word cloning became synonymous with making exact replicas of animals and humans; and most people outside of the scientific community did not realize that much less sensational versions of cloning—both natural and artificial—had been going on around them all of their lives.

The natural versions of cloning are virtually as old as life itself on the planet. In fact, the first and smallest life forms that appeared in the oceans over a billion years ago, each of which consisted of a single cell, reproduced themselves by cloning. The offspring of any living thing that reproduces by asexual means, that is, on its own without sexual union or aid from another individual, is a clone. The parent, or genetic donor, passes on its DNA

What Are Genes?

The process of cloning a living thing fundamentally involves and depends on the genes possessed by that plant or animal. In this excerpt from his book on cloning and genetic engineering, David Jefferis provides a basic definition for genes and tells how they can be engineered to improve a living thing.

Genetic engineering [is] the rapidly growing area of scientific research that tries to change and control the design of living things. To understand cloning, you need to know about the smallest parts of living things. In every one of the billions of tiny cells that make up the body, there are groups of chemicals called "genes." Each gene is a set of instructions that controls how a protein is made. There are thousands of different proteins. They carry out the work of the body, from breaking down food for energy, to helping brain cells communicate with each other. Genetic engineering can remove some gene instructions from one cell and place them in another. A plant may be given genes to resist disease carried by insects. An animal may have genes added to make it stay healthy.

(the key chemical that makes up the genetic material) to the offspring, which grows into a genetically identical duplicate of the parent. A good many of the most abundant and primitive creatures on earth still reproduce this way, among them all forms of bacteria, blue-green algae, most kinds of protozoa, and some yeasts. Every single member of these species in every corner of the globe is a clone of a clone of a clone, going back eons to the very first versions in the primordial sea. (That does not mean that the modern ones are identical to the ancient ones. Various factors, including mutation by radiation or other means, periodically change the DNA, causing the species to undergo tiny changes. Over time, such changes can significantly alter a species or even result in the creation of a new species.)

Water hyacinths reproduce by creating clones, or genetic duplicates, of themselves.

Even some more highly developed kinds of plants and animals can reproduce by cloning. The water hyacinth, for instance, often sends out thin stems, each of which can grow into a genetic duplicate of the parent plant. Each new hyacinth then clones itself many times and the process continues to repeat itself. It is a rapid and efficient process, as many sailors know. Colonies of thousands of cloned hyacinths sometimes choke coastal water passages, making it difficult for ships to get through. The hydra, a tiny animal that inhabits ponds, clones itself in a similar fashion, as the baby hydra grows from the side of its parent and then breaks away to become a separate creature. In addition, both starfish and planaria worms can reproduce by cloning. If a part of one of these creatures is severed, it will grow into a completely new individual with the same genetic make-up as the parent, a natural ability that greatly increases the chances that these species will survive.

Advantages and Disadvantages of Cloning Crops

Human gardeners and farmers began imitating nature by cloning plants at least four thousand years ago and possibly earlier. They learned to take a twig or a cutting from a plant and place it in a container of nutrient-rich earth. When roots began to sprout from the twig or cutting, they transferred it to the ground, where it grew into a new version of the old plant. By taking cuttings from the best and healthiest plants, people found that they increased their chances of growing many more healthy plants. They did not know of the existence of genes and DNA, of course, and so they did not understand the cloning principle they were employing. All they knew was that it produced beneficial results, which was good enough for them.

Some of what these ancient farmers produced through cloning was good for their descendants, including us, as well. A few kinds of grapes used today to make wines in Italy and some other parts of Europe are clones of grapes first grown some two thousand years ago by Roman farmers. Over the centuries, Italian farmers carefully nurtured and continued to clone these vines, passing their unique qualities down through the generations.

Many other fruits and vegetables popular today are also clones from the past. "Go to the supermarket and look at a pile of apples, particularly expensive ones," says popular science writer Daniel Cohen.

> They are all the same size, shape, and color. The apples didn't turn out this way merely because of the way the trees were fertilized or watered. The apples are clones. When you bite into one of those perfect-looking Delicious or Macintosh apples, you're biting into a clone.[6]

In the early twentieth century growers developed some of the many apple varieties popular in modern markets. But a few date from considerably earlier. Today, for example, trees that produce the tasty Cox's Orange Pippin apple are all clones of a single tree planted in the early nineteenth century. Similarly, some varieties of navel orange are clones of a hardy, juicy kind developed in southern California early in the twentieth century; and many Idaho potatoes are clones of an original potato plant grown in that state.

Producing food this way has both advantages and disadvantages. The advantages are plain: better-looking (and therefore more salable), better-tasting, often more nutritious crops. Cloned fruits and vegetables are also more time-efficient and economical to grow, since farmers do not have to rely on trial and error and the wide variation in quality inherent in natural varieties of these products.

The main *dis*advantage of cloning foods is that plants that are genetically the same have the same vulnerability

Italian farmers have been practicing cloning for centuries, cultivating grape vines first produced by ancient Roman farmers and nurtured and passed down through the generations.

to certain diseases. So a disease that can kill a certain fruit or vegetable will likely kill most or even all of its clones if it comes into contact with them. To guard against this disastrous scenario, some farmers take advantage of the fact that most diseases are highly selective and attack only one or a fairly limited number of species. These farmers breed two, three, or more slightly different varieties of a crop and then clone each of them. With such diversity, if a disease strikes one cloned line, it may spare the plants in the other lines.

Unfortunately, some critics say, not enough U.S. farmers are presently employing this strategy. American crops lack enough genetic diversity to keep them sufficiently safe from disease epidemics, argues reporter and science writer Keay Davidson. "Many U.S. crops . . . come from an ever-shrinking number of genetic types," he points out. "Big agribusinesses like

Do American Crops Need More Genetic Diversity?

In this excerpt from a March 1997 article for the Washington Times, *noted science writer Keay Davidson points out a real danger of cloning crops or animals on a large scale, namely increased susceptibility to disease. An entire crop or herd might be wiped out if its members are genetically the same, he says. And because there is presently not enough genetic diversity in many American crops, he argues that the government should mandate more such diversity.*

Genetically homogeneous species [those with the same genes] are especially vulnerable to sudden environmental changes: say, a mutated virus or climatic shift. One of history's worst disasters was the Irish potato famine of the early 19th century. It struck after the impoverished Irish grew dependent on a single variety of potato. When a potato disease wiped out the crop,

hundreds of thousands of people died. Countless more fled to the New World. . . . If farmers continued growing a diversity of genetic types, they would have alternate breeds to fall back on during a potato famine–type crisis. But diversity has waned over the past century in the United States. 91 percent of the different breeds of corn have disappeared, along with 95 percent of the varieties of cabbage, 94 percent of peas, 86 percent of apples, and 81 percent of tomatoes. . . . What's the solution? The White House should at least declare a "moral commitment" to genetic diversity in agriculture. Working with Congress, it could come up with financial incentives to encourage farmers to enrich their genetic harvest—say, by raising more than one type of corn.

limited types because they're easier to mass-pro-duce. . . . Diversity has waned over the past century in the United States. 91 percent of the different breeds of corn have disappeared."[7] For the moment, American farmers as a group feel that, despite decreasing genetic diversity, the potential huge advantages of cloning crops outweigh the potential disadvantages.

As a result of cloning technology, more than 90 percent of the breeds of corn once common in the United States have disappeared.

Attempts to Clone Frogs

By the mid–twentieth century, some scientists saw that cloning farm animals might have some of the same advantages as cloning crops like corn and apples. Such technology would allow farmers to choose their health-iest, most productive livestock—the cows that gave the most milk, for instance—and produce whole herds of these valuable animals. Cloning animals would also aid laboratory researchers who have a regular need for var-ious kinds of animals for experiments and tests. More

These cloned mice, part of an experiment performed at the University of Hawaii, represent three succeeding generations, all carrying the genetic blueprints of a single individual.

often than not, it is desirable to have all the lab animals in a test be as much alike as possible to ensure that physical and other differences in the animals do not affect and confuse the results.

Both farmers and researchers have been breeding animals for these purposes for a long time. But the traditional process, called selective breeding, is laborious, expensive, and sometimes produces undesirable results. Typically, a farmer selects two of his or her best animals—perhaps a prized bull and a cow that gives unusually large quantities of milk—and mates them. The hope, of course, is that parents will pass on their desirable genetic characteristics to their offspring. However, in any normal sexual union genes can combine in unpredictable ways; so the calf or calves born of the union may or may not be champions like the parents. Obviously, cloning would almost completely eliminate this element of chance. A farmer could ensure that a calf cloned from a highly productive milking cow would be another highly productive milking cow.

As desirable as cloning complex animals like cows might be, though, the first scientists who attempted it found the process far more difficult than cloning plants.

As early as the 1930s, Hans Spemann, a Nobel Prize–winning biologist, described how cloning might be done. Take an egg from a female animal, he said, remove the genetic material from its nucleus, and then insert into the egg the genetic material from a cell of the animal to be cloned. When the egg grows into an embryo, implant it into the uterus of a female of that species and in a few months a cloned offspring will be born. Spemann began some primitive cloning experiments; but he soon gave up, recognizing that the tiny instruments required, as well as much-needed knowledge of genetics, did not yet exist. "Decisive information about this question," he remarked, "may perhaps be afforded by an experiment which appears . . . to be somewhat fantastical. . . . I see no way [of successfully conducting such an experiment] for the moment."[8]

In the 1950s, two scientists picked up more or less where Spemann had left off. With the benefit of slightly better equipment and knowledge, Robert Briggs and Thomas J. King, working at Philadelphia's Institute for Cancer Research, were the first to remove the nucleus from a frog's egg and transplant into it the nucleus from the cell of an embryonic frog. (Frog's eggs and embryos were chosen partly because they are larger and therefore

Attempts to clone frogs occurred during the 1950s and 1960s, but the researchers were unable to produce adult frogs.

easier to work with than those of most other animals.) Unfortunately, the cloned frog embryo that resulted did not live long; nor did any of the others Briggs and King created in the months that followed. In the mid-1960s another researcher, Oxford University biologist John Gurdon, repeated the Briggs-King experiment and managed to produce tiny tadpoles. However, all of these died before they could mature into fully developed frogs.

Public Perceptions and Hitler's Cells

Today's scientists understand why these early experiments in animal cloning failed. The equipment Briggs, King, and Gurdon used was not delicate and sophisticated enough for the microscopic work involved, and the instruments damaged the genetic material of the cells. These cells could not grow normally, so the embryos and tadpoles inevitably died. But at the time, explains Princeton University biologist Lee Silver,

> most scientists interpreted Gurdon's essentially negative results differently. Rather than blaming technology, we blamed mother nature herself. In an almost religious way, we assumed the existence of a basic biological principle: adult cell nuclei cannot be readily reprogrammed back to the embryonic state. . . . It seemed reasonable to assume that it would never be possible to clone adult cells of more highly developed mammalian species . . . into healthy live-born children.[9]

But while most scientists were convinced that cloning higher animals, including humans, was impossible or at least centuries in the future, large sectors of the public were less pessimistic. Science had recently managed to overcome many seemingly impossible hurdles—the splitting of the atom and the development of vaccines to fight deadly diseases, for example. In the layman's mind, therefore, the successful cloning of a frog's egg, even if the embryo had not grown into a new frog, suggested cloning of higher animals, humans included, was not only possible, but also probable.

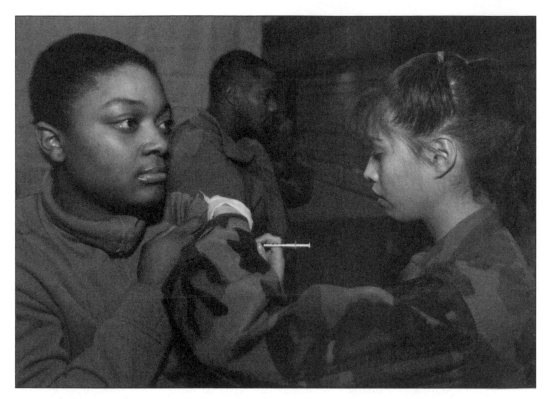

Bolstering this perception in the public consciousness, popular books and films explored and exploited the cloning concept. In 1970 Alvin Toffler's best-selling non-fiction vision of the near future, *Future Shock*, included this provocative passage:

The fact that vaccines have become an everyday reality has helped bolster the public perception that animal and human cloning is also possible.

> One of the more fantastic possibilities is that man will be able to make biological carbon copies of himself. . . . Cloning would make it possible for people to see themselves anew, to fill the world with twins of themselves. . . . There is a certain charm to the idea of Albert Einstein bequeathing copies of himself to posterity. But what of Adolf Hitler?[10]

Novelists and filmmakers immediately responded to these ideas. In 1973 comedian Woody Allen released *Sleeper*, a hilarious screen spoof in which someone in a near-future society attempts to clone a replica of a dead dictator from the deceased man's nose, which has been kept alive at great expense for almost a year.

In a much more serious, disturbing, and for many people very believable vein, in 1976 popular novelist Ira Levin published *The Boys from Brazil*. In this chilling story, Nazi doctor and war criminal Josef Mengele (who was a real person) manages to create ninety-four clones of the notorious dictator Adolf Hitler (from cells donated by Hitler before his death at the close of World War II). The boys, who are all physically identical, are now teenagers living in various parts of the world in families specifically chosen because they resemble the one in which Hitler himself was reared. (Here, Levin addressed the crucial point that copying the genes would duplicate only the dead person's physical attributes; to re-create personality and beliefs, one would have to reproduce his or her early environment and experiences.) The plan is to end up with at least one new Hitler, who will grow up to start a Fourth Reich and at last fulfill the Nazi dream of world conquest. However, as the story unfolds a noted Jewish Nazi hunter luckily uncovers and foils the scheme, killing the despicable Mengele in the process. In 1978 a film version of the novel, starring Gregory Peck as Mengele and Sir Laurence Olivier as his nemesis, was released to wide acclaim.

Gregory Peck (left) as Dr. Mengele and Laurence Olivier as his Jewish enemy in the 1978 film version of Ira Levin's The Boys from Brazil.

A Disservice to Science

Books and films like *The Boys from Brazil* almost always portray cloning as an example of science gone wild, a technique invariably used for silly, dangerous, immoral, or at least very questionable purposes. It was not surprising, therefore, that many people around the world were disturbed by the sudden report that a human had finally been cloned. In 1978, the same year the film version of Levin's novel about cloning Hitler was released, Philadelphia publisher J. B. Lippincott released a book by science writer David Rorvik titled *In His Image: The Cloning of a Man*. Supposedly, a very rich man, whom Rorvik called "Max" to conceal his real identity, had phoned the writer asking for help. Max, who was old, single, and desperate to have a biological child, asked Rorvik to find a scientist who would agree to clone him. Rorvik claimed that he eventually located a scientist, whom he called "Darwin," who succeeded in creating a clone of Max. The baby was supposedly born two weeks before Christmas in 1976.

The problem was that none of the reputable scientists involved in genetic research at the time believed the claim. It was far too difficult, they said, for anyone to clone a human, given the scientific knowledge and equipment then available; they concluded Rorvik's book must be a hoax. In fact, Rorvik never produced any solid evidence to substantiate his claim. And four years after the book came out, Lippincott was forced to admit that the whole thing was indeed a hoax (although the publisher denied knowing this when it had entered into the deal).

Though Rorvik and his book had been discredited, the hoax had done a great disservice to science in the general sense and more particularly to the notion and scientific potential of cloning. Before the hoax was revealed, television and the print media were ablaze with stories about cloning, most of which distorted information and had an alarmist tone. Meanwhile, a U.S. government official announced: "[If] the story is true, there should be an open hearing to lay the issues out before Congress and the public."[11] Such hearings did occur in April 1978. And most of the scientists who testified did not want to associate themselves with what the public and the politicians obviously viewed as a dangerous misuse of science. "In order to placate a skeptical public," science writer Gina Kolata explains,

> which was coming to see scientists as intrinsically untrustworthy, driven more by curiosity and a perverse glee in manipulating life than by moral qualms about what is proper and appropriate, some leading scientists found

Genes Not the Only Factor

Ira Levin's novel *The Boys from Brazil,* addresses a fundamental reality of human cloning—essentially the old argument about nature versus nurture. In the story, Nazi hunter Yakov Liebermann discovers that Nazi war criminal Josef Mengele has placed ninety-four identical-looking boys in families with similar backgrounds and circumstances. Puzzled and disturbed, Liebermann seeks the advice of a biologist, who explains to him the process of cloning, which as far as he knows is still only theoretical. Not yet aware of the identity of the person Mengele may have cloned (who is in reality the dead Nazi dictator Adolf Hitler), Liebermann asks if Mengele could have cloned humans as early as the early 1960s. The biologist replies that the theory was already known, and that all the Nazi doctor would have needed was the right equipment, good surgical skills, and some healthy young women willing to carry the babies.

The biologist further explains that genes are not the only factor in human development. A child created by cloning will grow up looking like his donor, he says, and sharing certain characteristics with him. But if he grows up in a different environment and is subjected to different cultural influences, he will almost certainly turn out to be quite a different person from his donor. Mengele was obviously interested in reproducing himself, the biologist suggests. The similar families with which Mengele placed the boys appear to be an attempt to increase the chances that they will grow up in the same environment he did and therefore turn out to be more like him.

themselves boxed into a corner. They had to argue publicly
. . . that not only was it untrue that cloning had been done,
but that it was ridiculous to expect that it *could* be done—
then or probably ever. And they had to convince themselves that even if cloning could be done, they had no
interest whatsoever in doing it. [12]

Not surprisingly, the years that followed witnessed
few scientific experiments related to animal cloning.
And for all but a handful of scientists in a few scattered
labs around the world, the idea of cloning higher animals, including humans, faded back into the "safer"
realm of science fiction, where the mad scientists and
other questionable types who perpetrated such schemes
were not real and thus could not actually hurt anyone.
The surprise was all the more stupendous, therefore,
when in 1996 a little lamb named Dolly came into the
world and turned cloning into a very real and quite
momentous scientific revolution.

CHAPTER 2

A Big Splash for a Little Lamb: The Creation of Dolly

The little lamb named Dolly, the first animal cloned from an adult cell of a living genetic donor, was born on July 5, 1996, at the Roslin Institute, in Roslin, Scotland. She was a true clone created in the institute's lab by a team headed by embryologist Ian Wilmut, who had used a cell from the udder of a healthy female sheep. This breakthrough, which electrified the world, was far from simple, sudden, or lucky, as some great scientific achievements occasionally are. A great deal of time, patience, and hard work went into Dolly's conception, mostly into developing the extremely sophisticated and specialized knowledge and techniques required to make it possible.

Embryonic Versus Mature Cells

Indeed, "possible" turned out to be the operative word in the whole affair. Throughout the 1970s and 1980s and well into the 1990s, the majority of scientists engaged in genetic-related research strongly suspected that cloning a higher animal and producing a healthy offspring was *not* possible. True, frog embryos and tadpoles had been produced in the 1950s and 1960s. But those experiments had involved a number of problems and limitations that did not make other researchers very enthusiastic.

First, the experiments in question had used the DNA from the cells of frog embryos, not a mature adult cell taken from a living frog. Demonstrating the ability to clone embryos was certainly important from a scientific standpoint. But it is basically no different than what nature already does when it creates twins or triplets inside the womb. As Daniel Cohen puts it:

> The researcher who is making clones from embryo cells is essentially creating more twins [of the embryo itself]. [By contrast] if an adult cell is used to make a clone, the researcher has essentially created a genetic copy—a twin, if you will—of a fully developed creature that already exists. [13]

For their creation to qualify as a true human-made artificial clone, therefore, scientists had to demonstrate that they could take a cell from a living creature and use it to make a duplicate of that creature.

Members of the press converge on Dolly at her birthplace, the Roslin Institute, near Edinburgh, Scotland, in late February 1997.

Another limitation of working with the frog embryos, or the embryos of any animal for that matter, was that for a long time it appeared to be too difficult, perhaps even impossible, to clone from an adult cell. The reason, scientists suspected, was connected somehow to the fundamental difference between embryonic and more mature cells. In simple terms, the more mature cells have become differentiated, meaning that each of them has begun to fulfill a specific purpose or function within the body. "The problem begins with the mysteries of embryo development," Gina Kolata explains:

> Every cell in the body arises from the same fertilized egg and so every cell in the body has exactly the same genes. But animal—and human—cells are specialized, differentiated, so that a heart cell behaves like a heart cell and a liver cell like a liver cell. The process of differentiation begins almost as soon as a fetus forms, and once a cell has reached

How to Clone a Sheep

In this excerpt from her book, Clone: The Road to Dolly and the Path Ahead, *microbiology expert Gina Kolata explains the basic physical steps the scientists at the Roslin Institute used to clone Dolly in the mid-1990s.*

To clone, [Ian] Wilmut used methods his research group and others had been developing for more than a decade. His colleague Keith Campbell sucked the nucleus out of an egg that had been removed from a ewe, creating an egg that had no genes at all, an egg that would soon die if it did not get a new nucleus. Then he began the process of adding the nucleus of an udder cell to the bereft egg. Campbell slipped an udder cell under the outer membrane of the egg. Next, he jolted the egg for a few microseconds with a burst of electricity. This opened the pores of the egg and the udder cell so that the contents of the udder cell, including its chromosomes [containing the genes and DNA], oozed into the egg and took up residence there. Now the egg had a nucleus—the nucleus of the udder cell. In addition, the electric current tricked the egg into behaving as if it were newly fertilized, jump-starting it into action. After 277 attempts to clone the udder cell, Wilmut's group succeeded and Dolly was created.

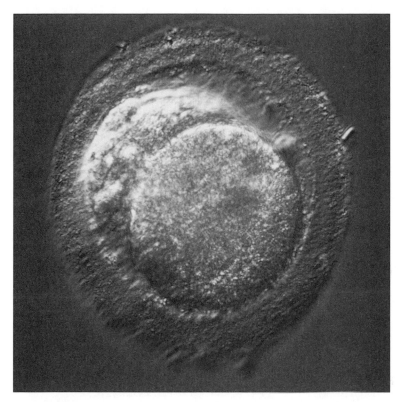

As the cells of this fertilized egg mature, they will become differentiated, or specialized to specific tasks within the body.

its final state, it never alters. A brain cell remains a brain cell for as long as a person is alive; it never turns into a liver cell, even though its genes are the same.[14]

The frog experiments and other research that followed seemed to indicate that primitive cloning of embryonic cells was possible; but once the cells had become differentiated, for reasons unknown it was no longer possible, or at least so difficult as not to be practical.

Living Drug Factories?

These were some of the formidable challenges that faced Ian Wilmut and his colleagues when they set out to clone sheep. The initial experiments began in 1986. The motivation was not simply to be the first lab in the world to clone a higher animal, but to provide direct practical benefits for farmers and indirect benefits for public consumers who buy what farmers produce. The Roslin Institute was founded during World War II at a time when the British Isles had been blockaded by the Germans, causing severe food shortages. The lab's original mandate was to use the fairly new field of genetics to produce more food from existing resources. In the 1960s the institute expanded its aims to include finding ways of making livestock healthier and more productive.

The experiments with sheep at the Roslin Institute that eventually led to Dolly were an extension of this idea of making domestic farm animals more productive. In this case, the researchers wanted to find better ways of using sheep to make drugs that might help fight human diseases, especially hemophilia (in which the blood does not clot properly, increasing the chances of a person bleeding to death) and cystic fibrosis (a glandular disorder that causes severe respiratory distress). Scientists had earlier found a way to genetically engineer sheep so that their milk contained a drug called alpha-1 antitrypsin. Because this drug had shown considerable promise in treating cystic fibrosis, it would obviously be beneficial and valuable.

The problem is that only a small quantity of alpha-1 antitrypsin can be extracted from the milk of a single sheep. And performing the genetic engineering necessary to make even a few sheep produce the drug is time consuming and expensive. Thus manufacturing alpha-1 antitrypsin in this manner would be prohibitive. On the other hand, Wilmut and his fellow researchers realized, if they could clone a sheep that had already been genetically altered to produce the drug, all of its offspring would be automatically programmed to produce it. "Cloned sheep could become living drug factories," in the words of one expert,

> and might produce valuable drugs much more cheaply than did the methods used by drug companies. . . . [The researchers] would clone a lamb whose udder cells made the drug whenever they made milk—all they'd have to do is hook the drug-producing gene to the gene that is turned on when milk is produced and make clones from those

genetically altered cells. Then the company could simply milk the sheep, extract the drug from the milk, and sell it. If the scientists made both male and female sheep that carried the added gene, they could breed these sheep and have a self-perpetuating flock of living drug factories.[15]

Megan and Morag

All of this sounded wonderful in theory. But at the time Wilmut and his colleagues began the project, no one had yet managed to clone healthy living animals even from embryonic cells much less from mature cells. The tadpoles created in the 1960s did not count, since they had not been healthy and had died long before growing into frogs. In 1981 two researchers, one from the prestigious University of Geneva (in Switzerland), claimed they had cloned three mice that had been born alive and healthy. They had done so, they said, by transplanting genetic material from a mouse embryo into a mouse egg. Though this was still only embryonic cloning, rather than cloning a living animal, it seemed to be an

The scientists at Roslin first succeeded in cloning sheep like this one from embryonic cells before they attempted to clone from the cell of an adult animal.

important advance, since mice are mammals and a good deal more biologically sophisticated than tadpoles and frogs. However, other scientists were unable to duplicate the results of this experiment. (Duplication of results is a crucial part of the scientific process; if an experiment cannot be repeated over and over with the same results, it is assumed that the original results were a fluke or somehow suspect.) In short, many experts came to believe that one or both of the researchers involved had faked the evidence.

Thus, Wilmut and Keith Campbell, a biologist at the Roslin Institute, realized that they had to learn to walk before they could expect to run. In other words, they first had to demonstrate the ability to clone a mammal from embryonic cells that had already become differentiated; if successful, they might then be ready to try the same thing with a differentiated cell taken from a live animal. The main hurdle was the same one that had plagued scientists for decades: How could they extract the DNA they needed from a differentiated cell? All previous experiments had suggested that such cells had genetically "switched off," so to speak, and were no longer viable for cloning.

Then Campbell had an idea. Maybe there was a way to slow down the cellular activity of a differentiated embryonic cell so that it would react more like a younger, undifferentiated embryonic cell. As science writer Michael Specter explains:

> Dr. Campbell decided that rather than try to catch a cell at just the right moment, perhaps he could just slow down cellular activity, nearly stopping it. Then the cell might rest in just the state he wanted so it could join with an egg. . . . What he decided to do was to force the donor cells into a sort of hibernating state, by starving them of some nutrients. In Wisconsin, Dr. [Neal] First had actually beaten the Scottish group to cloning a mammal from cells from an early embryo; that occurred when a staff member in the laboratory forgot to provide the nourishing serum, inadvertently starving the cells. The result, in

Because Megan and Morag were not cloned from an adult animal, the press seemed uninterested in them.

1994, was four calves. But even Dr. First and his colleagues did not realize the significance of how the animals had been created. Two years later, Drs. Wilmut and Campbell tried the starvation technique on embryo cells to produce Megan and Morag, the world's first cloned sheep. . . . Their creation really laid the foundation for what happened with Dolly.[16]

In retrospect, it is somewhat perplexing that the birth of Megan and Morag made barely a ripple in the press and the public consciousness. Wilmut, Campbell, and their colleagues had shown conclusively that differentiated cells *could* be cloned after all. This suggested that taking an adult cell from a living animal and cloning it was at least feasible. Wilmut and Campbell dutifully reported their results in the prestigious journal *Nature*. Yet save for a handful of interested researchers, few people paid any attention to the announcement. This lack of attention may be partly explained because Wilmut and Campbell had not actually cloned a living animal, and the public rarely understands or cares about the technical events and details leading up to a major discovery.

A Live Finn-Dorset Lamb

Unperturbed by the general lack of public interest in Megan and Morag, Wilmut and his Roslin colleagues forged ahead to the next logical stages of the project. "In the Winter of 1995–1996," Wilmut himself tells it,

> Keith [Campbell], Jim McWhir, Bill Ritchie, and I collaborated with Angelica Schnieke and Alex Kind . . . to clone lambs from three different kinds of cultured cells: from nine-day-old embryo cells; from fetal fibroblasts [flat cells similar to those found in the skin]; and from cultures derived from adult mammary gland cells.[17]

Working with the third kind of cell—which was taken from the mammary glands of a living sheep—was of course the crucial test. The future of cloning technology depended on whether the DNA from such a cell could be implanted in a sheep's egg and result in the birth of a new, asexually conceived sheep. About these crucial mammary cells, which came from a breed of sheep known as a Finn-Dorset, Wilmut continues:

> In the most important respects, the method was the one that we [had used] for Megan and Morag. We deprived the cultured cells of growth factor [i.e., nutrients] for five days to put them into the quiescent [hibernating] state. . . . Bill and Keith between them constructed 277 embryos from the . . . mammary cells. . . . Twenty-nine of them successfully developed into [larger, more advanced embryos]. These were transferred into [the wombs of] thirteen ewes [female sheep], of which one [belonging to the Scottish Blackface sheep breed] became pregnant; and this solitary Scottish Blackface surrogate mother went on to produce a live Finn-Dorset lamb. This was Dolly. . . . We did not immediately announce the birth of Dolly to the world at large. There were genetic tests to do . . . to ensure that the [lamb was indeed a clone of the adult donor sheep]. . . . We then had to write the account of what we had done. . . . It appeared in *Nature* on February 27, 1997, with the grand title "Viable Offspring Derived from Fetal and Adult Mammalian Cells."[18]

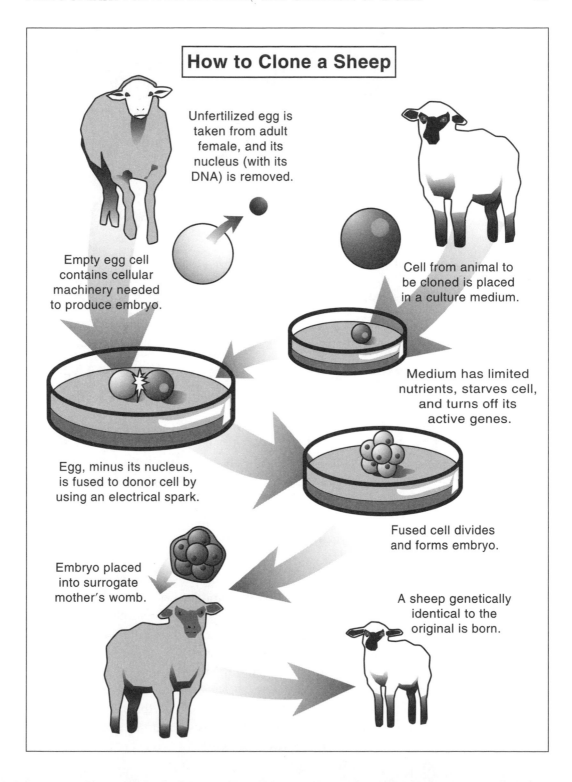

How to Clone a Sheep

Unfertilized egg is taken from adult female, and its nucleus (with its DNA) is removed.

Empty egg cell contains cellular machinery needed to produce embryo.

Cell from animal to be cloned is placed in a culture medium.

Medium has limited nutrients, starves cell, and turns off its active genes.

Egg, minus its nucleus, is fused to donor cell by using an electrical spark.

Fused cell divides and forms embryo.

Embryo placed into surrogate mother's womb.

A sheep genetically identical to the original is born.

A Scottish blackface sheep like the one pictured here carried the cloned embryo of, and gave birth to, Dolly in 1996.

Wilmut and the other members of the Roslin team were proud of their accomplishment and rightly so, for it marked a major milestone in the history of science. "Dolly has one startling attribute that is forever unassailable [beyond question]," Wilmut later wrote.

> She was the first animal of any kind to be created from cultured, differentiated cells taken from an *adult*. Thus she confutes [disproves] once and for all the notion—virtual dogma for 100 years—that once cells are committed to the tasks of adulthood, they cannot again be [capable of supplying the genetic material for creating another life]. The cell that created Dolly came from an adult ewe—indeed, the ewe that provided her genes was almost elderly—yet its ability to be reprogrammed into [the capacity to create a new lamb] was demonstrated beyond question. . . . All and all, Dolly is the stuff of which myths are made. Her birth was otherworldly, literally a virgin birth or, at least, one that did not result directly from an act of sex.[19]

"We Will See Ewe Again"

If the public reception that had greeted the birth of Megan and Morag had indeed been a mere ripple, news of Dolly's arrival generated a veritable tidal wave of reactions across the globe. Wilmut and his Roslin fellows fully expected a good deal of interest and publicity. "Nobody, however," Wilmut later recalled, "could have anticipated what actually happened."[20] In only the few days following the announcement of Dolly's birth, the small band of researchers was deluged by some two thousand telephone calls, nearly a hundred newspaper reporters, sixteen film crews, and over fifty professional photographers. Dolly was instant front-page news in virtually every newspaper in the world, as well as in *Time* and many other major magazines. (Whenever possible, the authors of the articles tried to come up with clever titles; typical examples included "Will There Ever Be Another Ewe?" "We Will See Ewe Again," "Spring Cloning," and "Silence of the Lamb.")

Nearly all of the articles, reports, talk show interviews, and so on made one point crystal clear: Dolly's big media splash had less to do with animal cloning and the benefits it might confer on humanity and much more to do

The Foundations of Biology Shaken

Here from his enlightening study of cloning, Remaking Eden, *noted biologist Lee Silver recalls the immediate and dramatic reactions of a thoroughly surprised world to the news of Dolly's creation.*

On the last Sunday in the month of February, in the third year before the end of the second millennium, the world woke up to a technological advance that shook the foundations of biology and philosophy. On that day, we were introduced to Dolly, a six-month-old lamb who had been cloned directly from a single cell taken from the breast tissue of an adult donor. There were lead stories on every television and radio news broadcast and headline banners on the front page of every newspaper around the world. And for weeks afterward, it didn't let up. Story after story came out discussing the stunning implications of this monumental achievement. On the streets, in offices, on campuses, and in classrooms, people couldn't stop talking about it. One little lamb had succeeded in changing our conceptions of life forevermore.

with where this new technology might lead. If an animal as sophisticated as a sheep could be cloned, went the general reasoning, human cloning must not be far off. On the one hand, some people were immediately enthusiastic and optimistic. Biologist Lee Silver later recalled how he was unable to sleep the night after he learned about Dolly. "It's unbelievable," he said. "It basically means that there are no limits" to what science might achieve.[21]

On the other hand, large numbers of people were disturbed by Dolly's existence. Many said so openly in

"Our Lives Would Never Be Quiet Again"

Here, from The Second Creation, *which he and his colleague Keith Campbell published in 2000, Ian Wilmut, leader of the research team that created Dolly, offers some personal feelings and insights about being at the center of a scientific revolution.*

Dolly has transformed my life. As the science and the technology that produced her are swept up into the grand stream of biotechnology, she will touch everybody's lives. Of course, as we waited for her to be born through the summer of 1996—not knowing whether any of the embryos we had made the previous winter *would* be born—I knew full well how important she was, and anticipated the impact she would make, although no one could have foreseen just what a fuss there would be or quite how frenetic [frantic] life would become. I suppose my mood through the summer was half-elated and half-fearful—fearful that we would fail to produce a lamb like Dolly, but also, from time to time, fearful that we *would* succeed. We are private people, Keith and I, not heading instinctively for the world stage (although I have discovered a taste for it), and I knew that our lives would never be quiet again. The world as a whole would be ever so slightly but ever so significantly different as a result of our endeavors.

Scottish researcher Ian Wilmut helped create Dolly.

print and live interviews. Another indication of this attitude was the sudden popularity of bioethicists, scholars who study and make judgments about whether certain aspects of scientific research are ethical or not. Before Dolly, the Internet website operated by Arthur Caplan, director of the Center for Bioethics at the University of Pennsylvania, received about five hundred hits a month. In the weeks following the big news from Scotland, that number jumped to more than seventeen thousand per day! Clearly, the concept of cloning had been elevated from science fiction to reality, creating a controversy in the process. And in the years since Dolly's birth, that controversy has shown no signs of subsiding.

CHAPTER 3

Of Cows, Pigs, and Rats: Potential Medical Benefits of Animal Cloning

When animal cloning became a reality in 1996–1997 with the creation of Dolly at Scotland's Roslin Institute, the new technology opened up a host of possible benefits for human industry and society. An obvious benefit for farmers and the food industry, for example, was the capability of creating entire herds of genetically engineered animals. Take the case of the nutritional value of cow's milk. Scientists already knew how to use genetic engineering to make a cow produce milk that is more nutritious than average for human consumption. (A certain human gene is added to the cow's own genes, which causes the milk to be more useful to humans.) Using the new technology that had produced Dolly, therefore, a genetically engineered cow might be cloned to make whole herds of cows that give the desired enhanced milk.

The potential of this approach for raising livestock was exploited almost immediately. Late in 1997, only months after the news of Dolly's birth stunned the world, a Wisconsin company, Infigen, cloned a bull, naming it Gene. Saying that the goal was to use cloning to aid dairy farmers, an Infigen spokesperson boasted that the company could make any number of identical animals possessing a desired trait. Since then a number of other similar companies have started up in the United States and other countries. For the moment, the technology to produce large animal herds by cloning is in the developmental stage and still very expensive. But the researchers involved believe that it will not be long before these companies will manufacture large numbers of cloned embryos of various kinds, each featuring some special trait, such as a cow embryo that will grow into an adult cow that gives more milk. Farmers will

Following the birth of Dolly, a number of other companies have cloned cows, sheep, and other farm animals.

leaf through company catalogues, choose the embryos they desire, order them by phone or the Internet, and then implant the embryos in the wombs of some of their existing cows. After a couple of years, such a farmer might build up a large stock of cows that give more milk than the average cow.

Cows, sheep, or other animals can also be genetically altered to be more resistant to certain diseases. Cloning such specimens could create large herds of animals less likely to contract such ailments. This is only one of the numerous potential medical advantages of the new technology. Indeed, many researchers and companies are especially excited about the possible medical benefits that human beings might reap from animal cloning. Among these are making useful drugs and effective medicines in large, relatively inexpensive quantities; growing animal organs for transplantation into humans; and increasing the efficiency of research into human diseases and their cures.

Treating Cystic Fibrosis and Emphysema

In fact, it had been the Roslin Institute's desire to make larger and less expensive quantities of the drug alpha-1 antitrypsin (AAT) that had led to the cloning of Dolly in the first place. That drug is used to treat cystic fibrosis, of course, and also emphysema, another disease that impairs the normal functioning of the lungs and causes severe shortness of breath. According to Ian Wilmut:

> Emphysema affects 100,000 people a year in Europe and North America alone. It is exacerbated [made worse] by insults [i.e., detrimental physical habits or effects] such as smoking, but the underlying cause is a genetic defect that leads to AAT deficiency. Cystic fibrosis is the most common single-gene disorder among Caucasians. An astonishing one person in twenty carries the defective gene, and one in 1,600 inherits this mutant gene in a double dose and then suffers from the disease. . . . The normal task of AAT is to counteract the effects of [an] enzyme, elastase, in the

Ian Wilmut (pictured) and others defend cloning animals, arguing that it will help scientists create the large quantities of drugs needed to fight diseases caused by genetic defects.

lungs. Elastase keeps the lungs flexible, but if it is not brought to a halt when its work is done, it attacks the lung tissue. In cystic fibrosis and emphysema, elastase does get out of control.[22]

Treating patients with these ailments by giving them the AAT they need to maintain normal lung functioning can be effective. However, before the advent of animal cloning, AAT had to be extracted from human blood plasma in the laboratory, which has several disadvantages. First, it is an expensive process. Second, using blood this way uses up precious quantities of an already limited supply needed for transfusions. And third, the process can be risky, since some human blood supplies are contaminated by serious diseases such as hepatitis and AIDS. In contrast, "pharming" AAT from herds of cloned animals would be cheaper, safer, and allow all of the blood supply to be used for other purposes. (Pharming, a new term combining the words "farming" and "pharmaceutical," means "the farming of drugs.")

Hope for Hemophiliacs and Diabetics

Hemophiliacs, people whose blood does not clot properly, are also certain to benefit from animal cloning technology. This disease is also caused by a genetic defect, namely a lack of the gene that orders the body to make factors VIII and IX, the proteins that cause blood to clot. Because one or both of these factors are missing from a hemophiliac's blood, he or she (although it occurs almost exclusively in males) can suffer significant blood loss, or even bleed to death, from a simple cut that would be relatively harmless to most people. The most common treatment for hemophilia is transfusion with blood containing the missing clotting factor or factors. Unfortunately, though, the therapeutic effects of such transfusions are only temporary. This is because the body is constantly manufacturing new blood and quickly replaces the blood containing the clotting factors with new blood lacking them.

Pharming by cloning may soon change the lives of hemophiliacs much for the better. As in the case of sheep and AAT, certain animals could be genetically altered to produce the clotting factors XIII and IX in their milk. Researchers and technicians could then separate the clotting factors from the milk (a fairly easy process) and make medicine for treating hemophilia.

The farming and dairy industries, which are of course the chief producers of milk, are already gearing up for the new technology. Herds of transgenic cows that can produce huge amounts of milk are already being created. (The term *transgenic* refers to an animal that has been altered to carry the genes of one or more other species besides its own.) "Milk is cheap, and we have an incredible dairy infrastructure"[23] says Carol Ziomeck, a scientist at Genzyme Transgenics, a genetic engineering company in Framingham, Massachusetts. Cloned herds will provide plenty of milk for pharming, therefore. As for genetically engineering the desired medicinal substances in that milk, there is no shortage of companies jumping on the animal-cloning bandwagon. According to a 1998 report in the prestigious journal *Science*, the potential of this technology has begun a sort of pharmaceutical "gold rush." As early as

October 1997, Genzyme Transgenics awarded Advanced Cell Technology [another Massachusetts-based genetic firm] a 5-year, $10 million contract to develop transgenic cows that will produce albumin, a human blood protein used in fluids for treating people who have suffered large blood losses. And in January 1998, Pharming Holding N.V., in Leiden, the Netherlands, formed an alliance with ABS Global, an animal breeding company in DeForest, Wisconsin, and its spin-off company, Infigen Inc., to develop transgenic cattle that produce the human blood proteins fibrinogin, factor VIII, and factor IX in their milk.[24]

The same approaches and techniques show promise for producing insulin, a hormone used in the treatment and control of diabetes. This condition, which affects one in twenty people in the United States, is characterized by decreased production of insulin by the pancreas and

Unlocking the Secrets of the Cells

In July 1997 Lester M. Crawford, director of the Georgetown University Center for Food and Nutrition Policy, testified before the House Subcommittee on Technology, which was investigating the new cloning technology that had recently produced Dolly. One of the potential medical benefits of animal cloning, said Crawford (quoted here from Gary McCuen's Cloning: Science and Society)*, is that scientists will be better able to study how somatic (adult, differentiated) cells work and behave. And this might lead to the prevention of many serious diseases and disorders.*

Studying the somatic cell nuclear transfer process [i.e., the cloning of a differentiated cell] itself in animals . . . could also provide other long-awaited answers [to previously puzzling scientific questions]. For example, so-called somatic mutations—mutations that take place in adult human and animal cells that are not inheritable—can cause tumors and other illnesses. Cellular changes of this type are also part of the aging process. Looking at the way cells undergo those sorts of mutations could help us better prevent cancer and avoid the negative effects of growing old, such as Alzheimer's disease. Ultimately, greater understanding of somatic cell differentiation might lead to the ability to regenerate or repair living tissue damaged by a variety of causes, including spinal cord injury.

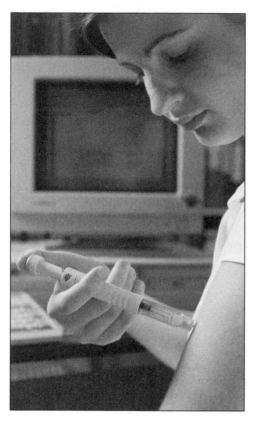

A diabetic injects herself with insulin. Cloning herds of genetically altered animals shows promise for creating large, inexpensive quantities of insulin.

unwanted increases of sugar and other substances in the bloodstream. Many diabetic people must take doses of insulin daily to avoid serious illness or even death. Cloning herds of animals that have been genetically altered to produce insulin would make it much faster and cheaper to manufacture the hormone than is possible using present laboratory methods. This would, in turn, make the insulin far more affordable for diabetics.

Animal Organs for Human Bodies?

Another area that promises considerable potential benefits from animal cloning is transplanting animal organs and parts, including hearts, kidneys, and bone marrow, into humans. A procedure in which a patient receives the organs of a member of another species is called a xenotransplant. Those unfamiliar with this concept might naturally ask why anyone would want to pursue it. Would it not be better to give a person who needs a new heart, for example, a heart harvested from a deceased human donor? The answer to this question is yes, at least in theory. However, the sad fact is that there are never enough human donor hearts and other organs for those who need them. It is estimated that as many as three thousand people in the United States die each year waiting for the donation of an organ for the transplant they desperately need.

Animal cloning might alleviate this problem, since large numbers of the right kinds of animals could be created for organ harvesting. But what kind of animal would be right for such a procedure? Monkeys, baboons, and other primates would seem to be likely candidates because their genetic makeup is similar to that of humans. In fact, in 1984 a California baby with a heart defect received a heart from a young baboon; and in 1995, doctors transplanted bone marrow from a baboon into a man infected with HIV.

In both of these cases, however, the recipients' bodies eventually rejected the foreign matter and the patients died. Doctors fully anticipate such rejection by the patients' immune systems. Indeed, the human body always rejects foreign organs, even those from other humans; that is why people who have received such transplants have to take dozens of pills a day to weaken their immune systems and thereby reduce the

Do Transgenic and Cloned Animals Suffer?

Not all people are enthusiastic about animal cloning, despite any possible benefits the new technology might bring human industry and society. Their principal concern is that the processes of genetic engineering and cloning are invasive, unfair, and ultimately harmful to the animals. Meg Gordon, a reporter for New Scientist, *a noted British periodical, summarizes these concerns in this excerpt from an April 1997 article for that journal.*

Now that cloning has the potential to turn a rare experimental procedure—the creation of transgenic animals—into a profitable, industrial process, ethicists, geneticists, agriculturalists, and animal welfare activists are warning that the new technology could encourage serious abuses of animal welfare. . . . It would be dangerous, they say, to allow the cloning of transgenic animals without first tightening up animal welfare regulations. . . . Bob Combes, a geneticist . . . at the University of Nottingham Medical School in Britain . . . is calling for an international committee to be set up to look at the welfare issues surrounding transgenic animals. He would like to see regulations which prevent companies from developing herds of transgenic animals until the long-term effects of each foreign gene on the animals' health have been fully assessed. "There are insufficient controls," says Combes. . . . [In agreement is] Caren Broadhead, scientific officer for the Fund for the Replacement of Animals in Medical Research, [who] says that genetic engineers "have no idea how [transgenic] sheep could suffer."

chances of rejection. Using such drugs faithfully, those who receive transplants of human organs have about a 75 percent chance of survival; whereas the odds are much lower for those who receive animal organs, which the body sees as even more foreign than human organs. In fact, Gina Kolata explains,

> the reason transplant surgeons [usually] steer away from using animal organs in humans, even though there is a dire shortage of human organs, is that animals are so genetically different than people. A pig kidney transplanted into a human is just so foreign that the person's immune system will attack it and destroy it.[25]

But what if an animal could be genetically modified so as to make its organs a better match for human bodies? "Scientists could take pig cells, for example," says Kolata,

> and add human genes to them in the laboratory, creating pig cells that were coated with human proteins. Then they could make cloned pigs from those cells. Each pig would have organs that looked, to a human immune system, for all the world like a human organ. These organs could be used for transplantation.[26]

This is exactly the course researchers at several companies are presently pursuing. The goal is to make transgenic animals by adding certain human genes to an animal's own genes in hopes that the animal's organs will be far less likely to be rejected by a human body. Kolata's use of the pig as an example is no accident; indeed, the pig is currently the animal of choice for this approach for two reasons. First, many researchers feel there is a higher risk of humans catching diseases from monkeys and other primates than from pigs. (This is because primates are for the most part wild animals, while pigs have long been domesticated and under human control.) Second, a pig's physiology (the size and shape of its organs) is very similar to that of a human. Scientist from Advanced Cell Technology in Massachusetts, Daniel Cohen points out, have

Cloning Animals Still Far from Perfected?

Some recent evidence suggests that cloning large numbers of healthy animals will be more difficult and take longer to perfect than previously supposed, as reported by science writer Gina Kolata in a March 25, 2001, article in the New York Times.

Scientists say evidence is mounting that creating healthy animals through cloning is more difficult than they had expected. The clones that have been produced, they say, often have problems severe enough—developmental delays, heart defects, lung problems, and malfunctioning immune systems—to give pause to anyone thinking of cloning a human being. In one example that seems like science fiction come true, some cloned mice that appeared normal suddenly, as young adults, grew grotesquely fat. . . . Leading cloning experts and developmental biologists said in recent interviews [that] the cloning process seems to create random errors in the expression of individual genes. Those errors can produce any number of unpredictable problems, at any time in life.

used embryo cloning techniques to make genetically identical pigs, and . . . also made trangenic pig clones bearing an extra human gene. The company hopes that it will ultimately be able to grow pigs with "humanized" organs that could be transplanted into people with less risk of rejection.[27]

More Efficient Research Animals

Still another potential medical benefit of animal cloning technology is to aid researchers who study human diseases and their cures. Modern science has always relied on the use of lab animals such as mice, rats, and guinea pigs to study how various diseases affect living creatures and to test new medicines that might fight those ailments. One of the problems with this approach is that the animals differ from one another physically and mentally, just as humans differ from one another in those ways. Through the time-consuming, tedious process of selective breeding, lab technicians can produce, say, fifty rats that are all white and about the same size and weight. But these rats are still genetically different. They came from different sets of parents and different litters; and they will exhibit slightly different habits and reaction times. Thus, a researcher conducting a drug test with these rats cannot be sure whether their reactions are mainly from the effects of the drug or from some unknown genetic differences in the animals themselves.

Cloning animals for research would not only virtually eliminate physical and possibly even most mental variation, but also, when used in conjunction with genetic manipulation techniques, open up new, much more efficient avenues for studying diseases. In the case of a researcher using cloned mice, for instance, one observer explains,

Cloning mice and other lab animals would eliminate variations due to genetic differences and make it easier for researchers to interpret the results of their experiments.

> genetic differences would not be a problem. All the mice would be identical. He would need fewer mice for his experiments, and he would know that whatever variations he saw were not the result of a genetic difference. [Furthermore] because it is possible now to add and sub-

tract genes from animals' cells, researchers could create animals that have the genes for a specific genetic disease. They could make, for example, a sheep with cystic fibrosis, then clone that sheep to produce [large numbers of] models of the disease for research. This might be a way to learn more about such diseases and how to treat them.[28]

It is important to emphasize that the animal cloning technology and applications described here are still in their infancy; and it will likely take several years to perfect them to the point where science and industry feel confident that they are completely reliable and cost effective. But there is little doubt that the practical ability to clone animals will revolutionize the fields of biology, medicine, and animal husbandry in the twenty-first century as much or more than the discovery of the germ theory did in the nineteenth century.

CHAPTER 4

Diversity and Dinosaur DNA: Cloning Endangered and Extinct Species

$\mathcal{S}$aving endangered animal species, those on the verge of extinction, is one of the most intriguing and far-reaching potential uses for the new animal cloning technology that created Dolly in 1996. In and of itself, extinction is a natural process. Over the eons, hundreds of millions of animal species that once roamed the earth or swam in the seas went extinct for one reason or another. Some of these reasons are explainable. The dinosaurs and numerous other species, for example, appear to have been exterminated by the catastrophic effects of the giant impact of a comet or asteroid 65 million years ago.[29] Other species die from more gradual causes, such as the inability to adapt to climatic and other changes in the environment. Still other reasons for the animal extinctions of the past are more mysterious; scientists have not yet figured out how they happened.

One common link all of these extinctions, explainable and unexplainable, have in common is that they were natural and therefore beyond the bounds of human control. By contrast, human beings themselves have caused numerous species to become extinct out of thoughtlessness, lack of foresight, apathy, or sheer greed. Overhunting various animals for their meat, hides, or horns; cutting down forests to clear the way for cities and roads; and poisoning the environment with toxic substances are among the major human causes of animal extinction. The giant ground sloth, moa (a large flightless bird), passenger pigeon, Tasmanian wolf, dodo bird, heath hen, and dusky seaside sparrow are only a few of the thousands of animal species destroyed by humans in recent times. Moreover, the rate of the carnage is accelerating. Thousands of species are on the endangered list. Experts estimate that as many as a hundred animal and plant species become extinct each day, most as the result of ever-expanding human civilization.

Dinosaurs like this T-rex became extinct some 65 million years ago. Many other species of animals and plants also disappear each year, and cloning could conceivably save some of them.

The dodo bird is one of thousands of animal species that became extinct in modern times.

These disturbing statistics point to a serious potential danger. Over the course of time, the unnatural loss of so many species might conceivably upset the balance of nature in harmful ways that no one today can predict. As scholar Jeanne DuPrau explains:

> Every time a species dies, whether it is a species of bird or plant, mammal or insect, the biodiversity of the earth is diminished. The word *biodiversity* has to do with the vast number of different kinds of living things that form an inter-connected web of life all over the planet, from ocean to mountain to desert. The connections are immensely complex. The loss of one species of insect, for instance, can affect the fish that feed on that insect, which in turn might affect the birds that feed on those fish, and the ecology of an entire river might be changed. No one understands all the intricate, complex connections among the millions of species on earth. But it is certain that the destruction of any one species can ultimately endanger all the rest, and that the richness and vigor of life on earth depends on its diversity.[30]

Cloning offers hope that the most seriously endangered species might be saved and the earth's rich biodiversity maintained. The creation of Dolly made it clear to scientists that new, healthy members of an animal species can be cloned from an existing specimen of that species. This might be possible even if the specimen is the very last of its kind. Moreover, some researchers are convinced that they might be able to take this beneficial scenario a bold step further. They point out that the genetic material needed for cloning does not have to come from a living creature. In theory, as long as the DNA is still intact the preserved cells of a dead or extinct animal might be cloned to produce a living duplicate of that animal. It might be possible, therefore, they say, to make the fictional concept behind the popular book and movie, *Jurassic Park,* in which researchers clone dinosaurs, a reality.

Saving the Enderby Cow

At first glance, these ideas might seem like flights of fancy. But remember that only a decade or so ago the idea of cloning an animal as complex and sophisticated as a sheep was considered impossible, or at least highly unlikely, even by most scientists. More important, once Ian Wilmut and his fellow Roslin researchers proved this gloomy forecast wrong by cloning Dolly,

The extinction of a single species like the grasshopper can have a rippling effect through the natural environment, altering the food supply and even the habits and longevity of the other creatures that feed on it.

other scientists wasted no time. A mere two years after Dolly's birth, cloning technology saved its first creature from the brink of extinction.

The animal in question was a rare breed of cow native to New Zealand. In the mid–nineteenth century, several cattle ranchers tried to start a ranch on Enderby, a small, barren island off the coast of mainland New Zealand. After only a few years, the ranchers abandoned the project and left. The cattle remained, though; and over the course of the century and a half that followed, their descendants adapted to the island's harsh conditions, undergoing distinct physical changes in the process. By 1992 one result of this evolution was a new breed of cattle. The other was a wild population of the beasts so large that it posed a threat to the island's ecology. Seeing no other practical choice, the country's government

Lady, the last surviving naturally born Enderby cow.

decided that the only way to save that ecology was to destroy the cows.

In the interest of science, however, a single Enderby cow was allowed to live. Agricultural officials shipped the cow, which they named Lady, to the mainland, so that scientists could study this new breed up close. After Dolly was cloned in Scotland in 1996, the New Zealand researchers decided to try cloning Lady to test the viability and practicality of using the new technology to save endangered species. Using a procedure similar to the one that produced Dolly, they took some cells from Lady's ovaries and grew them into embryos. They then implanted the embryos into the wombs of some cows of a different breed, which acted as surrogate mothers. The first calf was born in July 1998. This achievement showed that cloning could indeed become a viable method of saving endangered species.

Increasing Genetic Diversity

Biologists, zoologists, and other scientists around the world were extremely encouraged by the news of the success of the New Zealand experiment. One of these scientists was Kurt Benirschke, a biologist at and vice president of the San Diego Zoo, one of the leading sanctuaries of endangered animals in the world. In 1975 Benirschke began a program to freeze cells from endangered species. The original purpose was to preserve the cells so that their genetic material could be studied and compared to that of various similar species. But after the advent of Dolly, Benirschke realized that the cells he had been collecting might also be used to bring some endangered species back from the brink. "The possibilities for zoos are enormous," he remarked. "I would love to excite the international community to save as many cells as they can from as many animals as possible."[31] Moreover, the subsequent success of the New Zealand experiment has only reinforced his optimism. Oliver Ryder, a geneticist at the San Diego Zoo, agrees, saying, "I think [cloning] . . . offers the potential for a

To Save the Panda?

One endangered animal species that might be saved by cloning technology is the giant panda. A bearlike creature with beautiful black and yellowish white markings, an adult can weigh as much as 330 pounds or more. The giant panda is native to central China, where it usually dwells in cool, damp bamboo forests at elevations of five thousand to thirteen thousand feet. In fact, bamboo constitutes the main staple of its diet (although it will occasionally eat other plants, or if it is hungry enough, small animals). Because the bamboo forests are rapidly disappearing, thanks to encroaching human settlement, populations of giant pandas are dwindling. Only a thousand, and perhaps fewer, remain in the wild. A number of Chinese scientists are considering cloning the species to save it. They hope to create a giant panda embryo in the lab and then implant it into the womb of another animal, perhaps a dog, that will then give birth to a baby panda.

Chinese scientists hope to clone giant pandas like this one.

better safety net [for endangered creatures] than we thought we had."[32]

Ryder also foresees benefits of this approach that are not as obvious as simply saving a species from extinction. The new technology might actually be able to increase the genetic diversity of a dwindling species, he contends. On the surface, this suggestion sounds contradictory to one of the more popular images of cloning, namely that it will produce armies of genetically identical individuals. In other words, if the clones of a given animal are all the same, where is the genetic diversity? "For a species that are down to just a few surviving individuals," explains science writer Jon Cohen,

> clones grown from frozen fibroblasts [cells that form connective tissues and that are easy to grow in a lab] could provide an invaluable source of "lost" genes. Suppose scientists could clone Asian wild horses, South China tigers, or Spanish ibex [all endangered species] from cells in the [San Diego Zoo] collection that were gathered from long-deceased animals. . . . The clones [carrying the genetic information of these dead animals] theoretically would then be able to breed, reintroducing the lost genes back into the [existing] population [of the species].[33]

Ryder and other geneticists also believe that cloning will enable zoos to save animals that do not breed well in captivity. Perhaps the most celebrated example of such finicky breeders is the giant panda, only a few of which remain alive in zoos or the wild. In fact, a group of Chinese scientists has initiated a program to save the giant panda in the manner described by Cohen; they hope to achieve success within five years.

Some scientists want to create banks of cells taken from endangered animals like this South China tiger and, when necessary, use them to make clones to replenish the species.

All such experiments face various and sometimes formidable difficulties. First, egg cells must be removed from the animals to be cloned; and some scientists fear the process of removing these cells may harm these rare and sometimes fragile creatures. Second, even if the eggs can be safely removed and cloned embryos can be made from them, these embryos must be implanted into the womb of a surrogate mother. According to Cohen:

> Reproductive biologists say they would prefer to use females of a related, unendangered species as surrogate mothers so that females from the highly endangered population would be available for natural breeding. But it is not all that clear that the placenta carrying genes from the fibroblasts of a Rwandan mountain gorilla, for instance, would take [hold] in the uterus of a captive gorilla of a different sub-species. [34]

As Benirschke points out, however, such transfers of embryos from one subspecies to another have already been accomplished. An Angus cow carried the cloned Enderby calf, for example. And researchers from Ithaca, New York, and Suffolk, England, have succeeded in growing a zebra in the womb of a horse.

Bringing Back Beloved Pets

If the cells from deceased animals stored at the San Diego Zoo and elsewhere might be cloned to create living animals, might not *any* dead animal be cloned (assuming of course that its DNA is still intact)? Some people have already proposed cloning their dead pets, for example. There would be certain drawbacks to doing this, to be sure. First, though the cloned animal would look just like the original pet, it would not have the same memories, intelligence level, disposition, and so forth; so the owner would not really be bringing his or her pet back to life. Also, cloning is an extremely expensive process. So most pet owners would not be able to afford it.

For those who *can* afford it, however, it appears that cloning pets will become a real option before very long.

In 1998 an American millionaire paid some researchers $5 million to try to clone his dog. The experiment was not successful; but as Daniel Cohen points out, some new companies are betting the technology will improve and eventually become fairly popular:

> Geneti-Pet of Washington state has begun . . . freezing and storing blood samples of household pets in anticipation of the day when genetic technology may enable the deceased animals to be cloned. The company won't actually clone the animals, but it will store the blood in liquid nitrogen, where it can be kept in a near-perfect state of preservation at a fee of $200 a year until the time geneticists will be able to create clones from the blood cells. The company president says that he got the idea from ongoing scientific experiments to save endangered species. He figures the necessary procedures will become common within ten years.[35]

Some companies, including Geneti-Pet, in Washington State, have begun collecting blood samples from household pets, including dogs, betting that there will eventually be a demand to clone them.

The Dream of Resurrecting Dinosaurs

Assuming that deceased pets can and will be cloned, what about animals that have been dead longer? What about a creature that lived a hundred years ago? or a thousand? or tens of millions? This, of course, was the premise of Michael Crichton's very successful novel, *Jurassic Park*, which producer-director Steven Spielberg subsequently made into an equally successful film. In the story, a menagerie of dinosaurs, big and small, are cloned to populate a theme park on an island; unexpectedly, however, various things go wrong and the people on the island find themselves at the mercy of a bevy of bloodthirsty beasts.

Not surprisingly, the principal hurdle to leap in bringing such ancient creatures back to life is that no living specimens exist from which to take cells for the cloning procedure. To clone a dinosaur, one would need to find enough of its DNA still intact. But the remains of dinosaurs are so scarce and decomposed that managing to find any usable DNA will be an extremely daunting task. "Nature is an efficient recycler," experts Rob DeSalle and David Lindley explain:

An escaped T-rex *menaces paleontologist Allen Grant (played by Sam Neill) in Steven Spielberg's* Jurassic Park.

> Dead animals, whether in the Jurassic [period] or in your backyard today, are turned back into soil, plants, and other animals—which die and contribute their substance in turn to the next generation. It's entirely possible that our bodies contain atoms that once belonged to dinosaurs, arranged somewhat differently of course. . . . [That] explains why you're not likely to find any DNA in a fossil. DNA is

Some Dinosaur DNA Recovered?

As explained in this excerpt from The Science of Jurassic Park and the Lost World, *in 1994 some scientists from Brigham Young University thought they had found some dinosaur DNA; but it turned out to be a false lead.*

Scott Woodward and his team reported [in the journal *Science*] that they had removed fragments of dinosaur bones . . . estimated to be about 80 million years old . . . from a layer of stone lying above a deep coal seam. . . . The impervious nature of the stone, they believed had protected the bones from complete fossilization, allowing a little of the organic material to survive. In ultra-sterile laboratory conditions, they removed some DNA from this bone and concluded that it was not the DNA of any modern species. . . . Although that didn't exactly prove that it was dinosaur DNA, it seemed like a pretty good circumstantial argument. . . . If the DNA came from a dinosaur bone and looked unlike DNA from any modern creature, then the obvious conclusion was that it must be genuine dinosaur DNA. But Woodward's discovery was greeted skeptically from the outset. Many scientists believed that it was next to impossible to avoid contamination with DNA from other sources. . . . Woodward's case collapsed when several other groups of scientists looked more closely at the "dinosaur" DNA and discovered that it was a type that could, after all, be found in people. . . . Most scientists now believe that despite all his precautions, tiny snatches of human DNA got into the sample.

part of the organic [living] content that was replaced by rock [in the formation of the fossil]. It's gone—broken down and dissolved slowly into the swamp as the fossil formed, and ultimately recycled by nature into new plants and animals. Those atoms may once have formed a dinosaur's genetic code, but their provenance is completely obliterated.[36]

In his novel, Crichton got around this problem by having the scientists discover dinosaur DNA in dinosaur blood found in the stomachs of insects that had bitten dinosaurs. The insects had been trapped in amber (solidified tree sap) and thereby perfectly preserved for millions of years. The DNA of insects and plants some 30 million years old has in fact been found in amber. But it has been possible to recover only tiny fragments of the original genetic material. "The chances that the entire genome [genetic code] is still there, even in tiny pieces, seem remote," say DeSalle and Lindley. "Unless the preservation of DNA pieces is perfect, it just won't work. Even if only 1 percent of the DNA molecule is missing, no dinosaur."[37] Unless some presently unknown way to recover intact dinosaur DNA is discovered, therefore, cloning dinosaurs will remain an exciting subject for books and movies and nothing more.

"Pleistocene Park"?

Yet even if dinosaurs do prove to be "unclonable," that does not necessarily rule out the cloning of *every* prehistoric animal. Some ancient creatures who lived and went extinct thousands, rather than millions, of years

Paleo-DNA from Amber

In a key scene from Michael Crichton's *Jurassic Park*, some visitors to the park's lab receive an explanation from its chief geneticist, Henry Wu, about how he has managed to extract dinosaur DNA from insects trapped in amber. Tree sap, Wu explains, often flows over insects and traps them. The insects are then perfectly preserved within the fossil. All kinds of insects can be found in amber, Wu asserts, including those that might have sucked blood from larger animals, including dinosaurs. The visitors are intrigued and inquire whether this means that it might be possible actually to clone a dinosaur. With a wry smile, Wu then reveals that he and his colleagues have accomplished that very feat. He takes the visitors to a microscope, where a technician shows them a magnified image of a piece of amber containing a fly. On a video monitor, they watch him insert a long needle through the amber and into the body of the prehistoric fly. If the fly has any foreign blood cells, Wu explains, it may be possible to extract them and obtain "paleo-DNA," the DNA of an extinct creature. This is the work in which the lab has been engaged for the past five years, Wu adds. It has been a long, slow process, he admits, but it has paid off because the park now features living dinosaurs!

ago may well walk the earth once again. On occasion, the remains of skin and other soft parts from specimens of the woolly mammoth, an extinct, very large variety of elephant, have been found frozen in the icy tundra of Siberia. "The heyday of the woolly mammoth was the Pleistocene Epoch," explains scholar Richard Stone,

Some scientists say that ancient animals like this woolly mammoth could be cloned, provided that enough viable tissue can be found.

stretching from 1.8 million years ago to the end of the last ice age 11,000 years ago. Mammoths thrived particularly well in Siberia, where dry grasslands once stretched for hundreds of miles, supporting a vibrant ecosystem of mammoths, bison, and other jumbo herbivores [plant eaters]. They were in turn preyed on by cave lions, wolves, and saber-toothed cats. Famished after the end of the ice age by a diet of low-nutrient mosses, and increasingly harried by human hunters, the big grazers dwindled to extinction. Although most mammoths left behind only their bones, in a few cases the Siberian permafrost preserved mammoth skin and muscle. Most of the cells in this tissue had degraded, but in the past decade scientists managed to rescue a few proteins and fragmented genes to compare with those of living elephants.[38]

Based on these previous finds, a team of researchers is presently pursuing the dream of finding more intact mammoth tissue and cloning some of its cells to bring the species back to life. Japanese scientists Kazufumi Goto and Kazutoshi Kobayashi have already led more than one expedition to Siberia to search for mammoth remains. Their ultimate goal is to inject any intact mammoth DNA they find into the egg of a modern elephant (after the elephant's genetic material has been removed from the egg); create an embryo; implant the embryo in the womb of an elephant; and hopefully to deliver a healthy baby Siberian mammoth. Will Goto and his colleagues someday welcome excited tourists into "Pleistocene Park" to see walking, breathing members of species resurrected from the supposedly endless sleep of extinction? Only time will tell.

CHAPTER 5

The Advent of Human Cloning: Who Will Be Cloned and Why?

The cloning of Dolly at the Roslin Institute in 1996 did much more than open up new possibilities for increasing the efficiency of food production, making medicines, using animal organs for human transplant, and saving endangered species. The news of Dolly's birth also immediately raised the issue of cloning human beings. First, many people asked, if a complex mammal like a sheep could be cloned, would it not be possible, given sufficient time and some relatively small scientific advances, to produce human clones? Evaluating the techniques that created Dolly, many scientists quickly concluded that indeed—human cloning is not only possible, but also quite probable. This realization naturally raises questions about who will be cloned, and why, and how cloning technology might be applied to humans. Experts Eric A. Posner and Richard A. Posner sum it up this way:

No Fear of Mass-Produced Clones

In this excerpt from his book on cloning, popular writer Daniel Cohen explains why the once-prevalent idea that human cloning might lead to the creation of subservient or evil armies is easily dispelled and no longer taken seriously.

One of our darkest fears about cloning is the . . . image of hordes of clones produced for specific purposes, usually menial labor or warfare. Such fears come largely out of the misconception that cloned humans or sheep are actually "grown" in the laboratory. We have all heard the phrase "test tube baby." But that's not the way it [cloning] works. . . . To produce large numbers of human clones, given the high failure rate in cloning procedures, [very large] numbers of women would have to agree to undergo the repeated and sometimes risky surgery necessary to obtain eggs. Remember it took 277 tries to produce Dolly. Even more significantly, vast numbers of human surrogate mothers would be required. The number of women who would be willing essentially to rent out their wombs in order to grow clones is never likely to be very large. And the expense of producing even a single human clone would be enormous. It is far easier, safer, cheaper, and more pleasurable to reproduce offspring the old-fashioned way. That is not going to change. . . . The frightening image of mass production of laboratory-grown clones is now strictly science fiction, and will remain so for a very long time.

The news that a sheep . . . had been created by cloning adult non-reproductive tissue has given rise to speculation that it may soon be feasible to create human beings in the same way. In fact, substantial technical obstacles remain to be overcome, but [there is] no doubt they will be in time. . . . We assume that a safe and effective procedure will be developed that enables a man or a woman to produce a perfect genetic copy of himself or herself (or of his or her child—or anyone, for that matter), a copy that would bear the same genetic relation to the cloned individual that one identical twin bears to the other. We ask, who will want to take advantage of this procedure, and with what effects?[39]

The "Yuck Factor"

The question of who would want to clone either themselves or someone else used to be answered mainly with disturbing or nightmare scenarios dreamed up by science fiction writers. Mad scientists, dictators bent on world conquest, and other evil or demented people attempting to create armies of replicated humans were the usual visions conjured up by most people who considered the idea of human cloning. Now that cloning humans appears to be a real possibility, though, such extreme visions of human cloning have begun to give way to considerations of more realistic needs and uses of the procedure by everyday people. "In the years since Dolly," one authority on the subject comments,

> public discussions of cloning have shifted away from the specter of multiple human replicants to less disturbing possibilities, like the creation of genetically identical tissue grown for people with . . . [various diseases]. The initial revulsion at the very notion of cloning—what bioethicists call the "yuck factor"—has dwindled as more mammals have been cloned and as the prospect of someday replicating household pets seems to render the whole concept somehow cuter and more benign.[40]

Many people remain disturbed by the idea of human cloning for various ethical reasons. And the idea certainly raises a good many ethical and moral questions. But even most of those who are opposed to the human cloning do not worry that Dr. Mengele-like characters will breed hordes of evil followers to enslave humanity. (As bioethicist Arthur Caplan puts it, "If you want a mercenary army, hire one. Breeding one will take a long time and my hunch is that [because they will all be individuals with their own wills] they won't turn out to do what you want them to do anyway."[41]) In fact, in the years since Dolly's creation unleashed a flurry of research on cloning, those who have expressed serious interest in cloning or being cloned have almost invariably turned out to be quite ordinary people; moreover, the ways they want to use cloning seem to be beneficial or benign, though at the same time revolutionary or at least highly unconventional.

Bringing Back the Deceased

The word *unconventional* certainly describes one of the most common motivations cited by those interested in human cloning—bringing back deceased loved ones. Just as some people contemplate resurrecting beloved pets, others have expressed the desire to create clones of lost husbands, wives, children, or other relatives. Margaret Talbot, a journalist for the *New York Times*, tells the story of a couple who recently lost a child and are determined to replace him by cloning:

> Last year [in 2000] a ten-month-old baby boy died in the hospital after a minor operation went wrong. The baby's parents, an American couple, had two other children and probably could have had another if they wished; neither parent was infertile, and both were healthy and in their 30's. But they did not want another child. They wanted *this* child. And before long they began to believe that the longing they felt was telling them something quite specific—that their dead baby's genes were crying out, as a ghost might, to express themselves again in this world. The idea preoccupied them that their little son's genotype [genetic makeup] deserved another chance, that it had disappeared by mistake and could be brought back by intention.[42]

As strange as it may seem to some people, this is far from an isolated case. The number of people who express similar longings to clone deceased loved ones is steadily growing. Marion Vuchetich, a retired teacher, is one of them. Her son, Matthew, died in an accident in 1998 at the age of thirty-seven, and she would like to see cloning bring him back. Messages voicing similar sentiments continually flood Internet

Some parents who have lost young children have already expressed a desire to see those children cloned. Scientists point out that such clones would be only physical duplicates, since the mind and memories cannot be cloned.

websites like the Human Cloning Foundation (in Atlanta, Georgia), a group that promotes the concept of human cloning. "My wife and myself miss him so much," writes "David" of his recently deceased eight-year-old son in a typical on-line plea. "How would it be if there was a way to start all over again?"[43]

The idea that the clone of a dead person will be a complete replica of that person is a misconception, however. As those familiar with the technology often point out, cloning a person will duplicate only his or her physical appearance and other genetic elements, not the person's personality and memories. Will awareness of this fact make those desiring the procedure change their minds? To find out, Talbot interviewed several such individuals, including a scientist working with the young couple who lost their ten-month-old son. "Did the parents realize that even a baby who shared the original's genotype would not be the same person?" Talbot asked. "He'd be gestated in a different womb. He'd be subject to different environmental influences. And he'd be reared by parents who had been irrevocably altered by the loss of a baby."[44] In other words, the child would have his own mind because the human mind—consisting of an individual's unique personality, thoughts, memories, and emotions—cannot be cloned or otherwise reproduced. Talbot was surprised by how those she interviewed responded. "The odd thing, as I found out," she says,

> is how many people know this and don't know it at the same time. They will tell you that they realize that cloning does not produce a copy of the original person, but something more like a later-born identical twin, and yet [they] say that they would want to do it anyway. They'd want to do it so that they could know as much as possible in advance about their unborn children, so they wouldn't have to take their chances on sexual reproduction, so they could perpetuate their own genes or so they could hope against hope to get back somebody very, very much like somebody they had lost.[45]

Helping Infertile Couples

Whether one agrees or disagrees with the cloning of deceased people, everyone can agree that the actual beneficiaries of such a procedure are not the dead, but their living relatives. In fact, many scientists argue that human cloning holds the potential for helping the living in several more concrete and less controversial ways. The first is providing an alternative method for infertile couples to have a child genetically related to themselves (as opposed to adopting). "I think cloning has basically one real scientific use," says Lee Silver, "which is to overcome infertility and it can be used by people who are unable to produce sperm or eggs and it can allow them to have a biological child."[46]

At present, one of the two main alternative ways of having a biological child is in vitro fertilization, in which a woman's egg and a man's sperm are joined in the lab instead of within her womb; however, this method does not work for everyone. The second technique is used in cases in which a woman's eggs or man's sperm are defective or nonexistent. If the man is infertile, for example, the couple can accept sperm donated by another man, which combines with the woman's egg to produce a child. The drawback of this method, obviously, is that the baby will carry the genes of only one of the parents.

Once perfected, cloning would eliminate some of these problems. In the case of an infertile man, for instance, his genetic material could be extracted from some of his cells and transplanted into his mate's egg. Dartmouth College scholar Ronald Green also sees how human cloning would help two other groups of

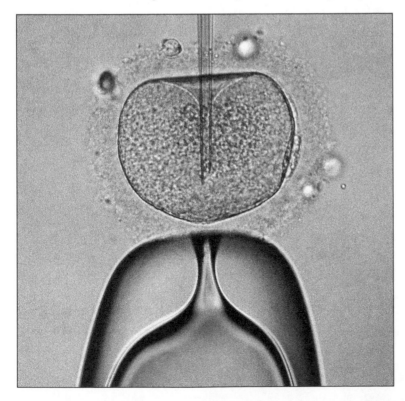

This microscopic view shows the process of in vitro fertilization.

people for whom biological children have not usually been an option. One, Green says, is "lesbian parents—and, to a lesser extent, gay men." (It would be lesser in the case of two gay men because they would still need a female surrogate to carry the child.) The other group, says Green, would consist of

> people with serious genetic disorders that are not amenable to other modes of prevention [i.e., preventing their infants from inheriting these disorders] like genetic screening—because maybe the specific mutation isn't known or many different genes are involved—and who still want to have their own biological child. [47]

After reviewing the possibilities of this potential new alternative method of having babies, Talbot remarks: "For some people, cloning just seems like a chance to

Gay couples might benefit from cloning technology, since it would allow them to have biological children of their own.

Cloning to Avoid Genetic Defects

A number of different kinds of couples might want to avail themselves of cloning technology to have children. Couples that are infertile, for instance, might want to choose cloning as an alternative to other means of achieving pregnancy, such as in vitro fertilization. Another kind of couple that might benefit, bioethicist Ruth Macklin explains in this excerpt from a 1997 article for U.S. News & World Report, *is*

a couple in which the husband has some tragic genetic defect. Currently, if this couple wants a genetically related child, they have four not altogether pleasant options. They can reproduce naturally and risk passing on the disease to the child. They can go to a sperm bank and take a chance on unknown genes. They can try in vitro fertilization and dispose of any afflicted embryo—though that might be objectionable, too. Or they can get a male relative of the father to donate sperm, if such a relative exists. This is one case where even people unnerved by cloning might see it as not the worst option.

have a baby with some kind of genetic connection—even if it's only one parent, even if the connection is uncomfortably close, even if they're a little vague on what a clone is."[48] Lee Silver agrees, saying:

I predict that in twenty years, when this fuss [i.e., the controversy about the possible harmful aspects of human cloning] has died down and we understand what cloning can do and what it can't do, it will be just one more reproductive technique, like in vitro fertilization, to help infertile people have babies.[49]

A Medical Revolution?

Besides infertile couples, say a number of researchers, people with serious medical conditions or problems will avail themselves of human cloning technology. This approach would utilize the technology in ways that would not involve creating new human beings. Instead, replacement organs and tissues for sick or injured people would be grown in the lab "to order" for the specific patients who need them. Although using cloning to produce animal organs for human transplants certainly shows promise, that technique still features the problem of rejection by the immune system, which means that this approach will ultimately fail in a certain percentage of patients. However, if the patient's *own* cells could be used to grow the organs or tissues, the match would be genetically perfect and no rejection would occur. Virtually all life saving transplants would succeed.

The cloning techniques for growing human organs and tissues will build on noncloning research pioneered by American and English scientists beginning in 1981. They knew that normally, as embryos grow and develop, their cells eventually begin to differentiate; some cells become heart cells, others skin cells, and still others bone marrow cells; and together, they grow into a human fetus, which later becomes a baby. What the researchers managed to do was to stop the normal development process at the embryonic level. The cells of the embryo continued to divide and grow, but only into more undifferentiated embryonic cells. These special cells came to be called embryonic stem cells, or ES cells for short. Lee Silver explains the tremendous medical potential of this breakthrough:

> What ES technology provides is a tool for expanding the embryo into a mass of undifferentiated tissue of any size that is needed. After this first step is accomplished, it then becomes possible to convert this undifferentiated mass into the particular tissue that one desires. . . . Just as certain signals can be used to fool ES cells into remaining in an embryonic state, other signals can be used to force them down specific pathways of differentiation in a controlled manner. Some signals might be used to turn them into bone marrow cells and others could be used to turn them into primitive nerve cells, for example. And what will almost certainly happen over the next twenty years is that scientists will discover what signals are needed to convert embryonic cells into every tissue that exists in the adult human body.[50]

To see how the ability to clone might be combined with this ES cell technology to work a medical wonder, imagine a little girl who has leukemia (a blood disease that is usually fatal). A bone marrow transplant could save her life. But finding a close genetic match of marrow from the list of potential human donors is difficult and sometimes fails. Moreover, even if such a match can be found, the risk of rejection still exists. So the doctors opt to take a cell from the girl's skin and clone it, producing a primitive embryo. Using molecular signals, they direct the embryonic cells to grow into a mass of ES cells and then convert these into bone marrow cells. When enough of the bone marrow cells have been cultured, the doctors transplant them into the girl; and because the new marrow carries her own unique genetic code, no rejection occurs; her leukemia is cured and she faces the prospect of a long and healthy life.

Such transplants may prove only the beginning of a virtual medical revolution based on the marriage of the ES cell and cloning technologies. New, healthy skin for burn victims, as well as brain cells for brain-damaged

Scientists argue that cloning technology may have many medical benefits, including producing healthy skin to heal burn victims.

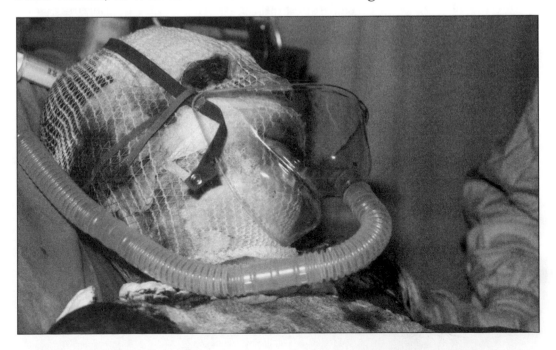

people and spinal cord cells for paraplegics, might be grown and transplanted. Hearts, lungs, kidneys, bladders, and other organs could be made to order for specific patients, saving or extending their lives. The possibilities and results of plastic, reconstructive, and cosmetic surgery would be significantly enhanced. And by learning how to switch cells off and on and redirect their development, cures for most or all types of cancer might be found.

The Race to Clone a Person

Assuming such medical advances and benefits will truly be possible, when will they become a practical reality? That question is too difficult to answer at present, mainly because human cloning research is still in its very early stages. The first major step—cloning human embryos—has already been taken. In December 1998 a team of scientists in a lab in Seoul, South Korea, succeeded in creating such an embryo consisting of a few cells. (They then destroyed the embryo for reasons that are unclear.) The experiment has been repeated in various other labs since that time. Taking the next steps in the process of human cloning—implanting the embryos in human wombs and safely growing them to term—will not be easy. But they will certainly be feasible considering the constantly improving state of medical and reproductive technology. According to Silver, one of the leading researchers in the field:

> It requires only equipment and facilities that are already standard or easy to obtain by biomedical laboratories and free-standing in vitro fertilization clinics across the country and across the world. Although the protocol [procedure] itself demands the services of highly trained and skilled personnel, there are thousands of people with such skills in the United States alone.[51]

In fact, at least two teams of researchers are presently engaged in full-scale efforts to clone human beings. (Two have announced they are doing so, but others may well be working in secret and planning to reveal their programs only if and when they succeed.) One of these teams, headed by Brigitte Boisselier, a French chemist, is connected with the Raëlians, a UFO cult based in Quebec, Canada. The group's spiritual leader, who calls himself Raël, claims to have been contacted by aliens, who told him that long ago they had created the human race through cloning. In this scenario, therefore, all human beings (including everyone alive today) carry extraterrestrial genetic material.

The Raëlians recently established a genetic research company, Clonaid, dedicated to helping infertile couples have biological offspring and to promoting cloning research in general. They are funded by private sources, including the earlier mentioned parents who want to

The Raëlians and Their Beliefs

In this excerpt from an article in the New York Times Magazine, *Margaret Talbot, a fellow of the New America Foundation, provides a thumbnail sketch of the Raëlians, the Canadian UFO group whose genetics lab is presently a frontrunner in the race to be the first to clone a human being.*

The Raëlians are not a tiny group—they claim 55,000 members worldwide, though the number is probably closer to 25,000, according to Susan Palmer, a sociologist who has studied them. And they are not without resources. Since 1974, they have raised $7 million toward the construction of an "embassy" where alien visitors could be welcomed to our planet in style. Their followers, who hold fast to the ideal of everlasting life created through technology, are a devoted lot. Their leader has, in the words of Charles Cameron, a researcher with the Center for Millennial Studies at Boston University, "done an extremely good job of placing himself astride a powerful tide of hope and fear— the longings of people who want to find emotional and religious meaning in science and biotechnology.". . . [The group's leader is] Raël, a French-born former race-car driver. . . . In 1973, Raël says, he had an encounter with a four-foot-tall alien . . . whose flying saucer had landed atop a volcano in southern France. From this creature, he heard the message that humans had been created in a laboratory by advanced beings from another planet who had mastered genetics and cell biology.

bring back their son who died at the age of ten months in 2000. Once up and running, Clonaid plans to maintain itself by charging $100,000 or more per couple for its services. Most people, especially scientists, view the Raëlians as part of society's ever-present lunatic fringe, at least in regard to their unorthodox beliefs. However, a large number of reputable biologists and geneticists say the group has the necessary technical means at its disposal and must be taken seriously in the race to clone humans.

The other leading team in that race is headed by Panos Zavos, of the Kentucky Center for Reproductive Medicine, and Italian scientist Severino Antinori. Their cloning project, which is also privately funded, is proceeding at an undisclosed location outside of the United States. Like the Raëlians, Zavos and Antinori feel that the benefits of cloning humans will far outweigh the risks and also any ethical objections raised by those who disagree with using the technology. Says Raël:

> You can call it eugenics [the attempt to improve the hereditary makeup of humans], but not in a bad way, like the Nazi way of thinking before, which results in a superior race. No, cloning would be available to all human beings, to improve their characteristics and possibilities.[52]

A good many people fear that this outlook may be too optimistic, however. They continue to raise ethical and moral objections to human cloning, believing that it might be harmful to both individuals and society in various ways; and therein lies the controversy and debate that currently threatens to slow or stall large-scale scientific efforts to clone humans.

CHAPTER 6

Playing God?: Ethical and Moral Concerns About Human Cloning

Simmering in the background of all the present cloning research is a growing and profound debate about whether cloning humans is a road humanity should eagerly take or cautiously and righteously avoid. The opinions on both sides of the issue are so strongly held and voiced that the simmering threatens to come to a boil when the first cloned human is announced in the near future, an event that almost everyone involved in the debate sees as highly likely.

On one side are outright opponents of human cloning, who say it is unethical, immoral, potentially harmful, and should never be attempted. On the opposite side are those who find no particular moral problems with the technology and advocate actively pursuing it for the many benefits it promises for humanity. A third group in the debate lies somewhere in the middle. Its members are not fundamentally against the concept of cloning people but do feel that science and society should proceed slowly and with extreme caution to make sure it is safe for those who are cloned and does no measurable harm to society itself.

Cloning May Create Abnormal Offspring

Dozens of separate arguments against human cloning have been advanced by opponents and rebutted by advocates. But most of these arguments can be conveniently collected into groups with similar themes. One such theme revolves around the safety issue. Opponents say that the technology to clone humans is far from perfected and may never be. "All sorts of things go wrong," insists George Sidel, a cloning researcher at Colorado State University, in reference to the animals that have been cloned so far in labs around the world.

> Normally you might expect a 100-pound birthweight in a calf, but with a clone, you might get 160 pounds. . . . Sometimes the kidneys aren't right, they're just plain put together wrong—or the heart is, or the lungs, or the immune system. It can be a unique abnormality in each case. They can die within a few days after birth, or sometimes they just can't make it after you cut the umbilical cord.[53]

Indeed, some recent evidence does reveal sporadic physical problems with some of the mammals that researchers around the world are presently cloning. Some scientists involved believe a main cause of such abnormalities is that the genetic reprogramming of the egg in the cloning process may be happening too fast. In the course of normal reproduction, it may take months for an egg to program itself, that is, to "put all its genes in order." With cloning, however, says Rudolph Jaenisch, a biology professor at the Massachusetts Institute of Technology, "you are asking an egg to reprogram in minutes or, at most, in hours." This may introduce random errors into the clone's DNA that may lead to physical abnormalities. To proceed with human cloning at present would therefore "be reckless and irresponsible," warns Jaenisch. "What do you do with humans who are born with half a kidney or no immune system?"[54]

Those who say that human cloning *should* proceed right away argue that cloning technology, like any new technology, will inevitably get better, more precise, and safer as time goes on. They also say that opponents of cloning are asking for an unrealistic level of safety.

Could Cloning Halt Human Evolution?

According to Michael Mautner, a professor of chemistry at the University of Canterbury at Christchurch, New Zealand, one potential danger of human cloning is that it might severely limit the genetic diversity that arises from normal sexual reproduction. In this excerpt from a 1997 article for The Futurist, *he warns that this might have serious consequences for the human race.*

Cloning is not only less fun than sex, it would freeze evolution and destroy our chances for survival in the future. . . . Cloning on a large scale would . . . reduce biological diversity, and the entire human species could be wiped out by some new epidemic to which a genetically uniform population was susceptible. . . . In sexual reproduction, some of the genetic material from each parent undergoes mutations that can lead to entirely new biological properties. Vast numbers of individual combinations become possible, and the requirements of survival—and choices of partners by the opposite sex—then gradually select which features will be passed on to the following generations. . . . Cloning will, in contrast, reproduce the same genetic make-up of an existing individual. There is no room for new traits to arise by mutation and no room for desirable features to compete and win by an appeal to the judgment of the opposite sex. The result: Human evolution is halted. . . . Without the satisfactions of love and sex, of dating and of families, will cloned generations even care to propagate further? Cloning therefore raises fundamental questions about the human future. Have we arrived yet at perfection? Where should we aim future human evolution? What is the ultimate human purpose? The prospect of human cloning means that these once-philosophical questions have become urgent practical issues.

Advocates point out that even ordinary natural reproduction is far from safe. Miscarriages happen all the
time, as do stillborn babies, overweight or underweight
babies, babies with all manner of birth defects, and so
forth. Yet no one calls for a halt in natural procreation
(reproduction) because of safety concerns. "People
exaggerate the fears of the unknown," argues
University of Alabama philosophy professor Gregory
Pence,

> and downplay the very real dangers of the familiar. In a
> very important sense, driving a car each day is far more
> dangerous to children than the new form of human repro-
> duction under discussion here. Many, many people are
> hurt and killed every day in automobile wrecks, yet few
> people consider not driving.[55]

Living Up to Parents' and Society's Expectations

Another prevalent argument against the notion of
cloning people is that, even if those who are cloned turn
out to be physically normal, they may suffer harmful
psychological damage in various ways. First, it is
wrong, opponents say, to bring a child into the world as
a means for others' ends. Take, for example, the cases of
parents who might want to bring back dead children by
cloning, or to clone children with genetic alterations that
will hopefully make them smarter, more beautiful, or
more athletic. Such parents, say opponents, are merely
fulfilling their own selfish desires; and they may end up
disrespecting or even abusing or abandoning their children if they do not live up to their expectations. Indeed,
say some of those against human cloning, society in
general may have certain expectations of and discom-
forts with cloned children and treat them as inferiors or
outcasts.

The opposite of this argument is that such apprehen-
sions are misplaced, since parents' and society's high
expectations of some children is nothing new. According
to Harvard University scholar R. C. Lewontin, cloning

would not "significantly increase the already immense number of children whose conception and upbringing were intended to make them instruments of their parents' frustrated ambitions, psychic fantasies, desires for immortality, or property calculations."[56] Lee Silver adds:

Cloning proponents say that parents' controlling children before birth would be little different from controlling them after birth.

> There are those who will argue that parents don't have the right to control the characteristics of their children-to-be. . . . But American society, in particular, accepts the rights of parents to control every other aspect of their children's lives from the time they are born until they reach adulthood. If one accepts the parental prerogative after birth, it is hard to argue against it before birth, if no harm is caused to the children who emerge.[57]

Will Clones Suffer a Loss of Individuality?

But what about the issue of a cloned person's individuality? Might such a person lack or lose some of those essential qualities and feelings that make him or her different from everyone else? "Cloning creates serious issues of identity and individuality," asserts Leon Kass, professor of bioethics at the University of Chicago.

> The cloned person may experience concerns about his distinctive identity, because he will be, in genotype and appearance, identical to another human being; but in this case it will be a twin who might be his father or mother. What would be the psychic burdens of being the child or parent of your twin? Moreover, the cloned individual will be saddled with a genotype that has already lived. He will not be fully a surprise to the world, and people are likely always to compare his performances in life with those of his alter ego. . . . Genetic distinctiveness symbolizes the uniqueness of each human life and . . . can also be an important support for living a worthy and dignified life.[58]

Responding to this view, noted Harvard University professor and scientist Stephen Jay Gould makes the case that a cloned person would be significantly more genetically distinct and unique than millions of people alive today. Namely, he is talking about identical twins.

Paleontologist Stephen Jay Gould argues that identical twins are human clones that have been around since time began.

"We have known human clones from the dawn of our consciousness," he says. "We call them identical twins." In the following comments, Gould uses Dolly and her mother (and DNA donor) to draw comparisons between clones and identical twins.

Dolly only shares nuclear DNA with her mother's mammary cell. . . . Dolly then grew in the womb of [a female] surrogate. Identical twins share . . . important attributes that differ from Dolly and her mother. Identical twins share the same set of maternal gene products in [the fluid portion of] the egg . . . [while] Dolly has her mother's nuclear genes, but her surrogate's gene products. . . . Identical twins [also] share the same womb. Dolly and her mother gestated in different places. [In addition] identical twins share the same time and culture. . . . The clone of an adult cell matures in a different world. . . . So identical twins are truly eerie clones—ever so much alike, on all counts, than Dolly and her mother. We do know that identical twins share massive similarities, not only in appearance, but also in . . . detailed quirks of personality. Nonetheless, have we ever doubted the personhood of each member in a pair of identical twins? Of course not. We know that identical twins are distinct individuals, albeit with peculiar and extensive similarities. We give them different names. They encounter divergent experiences and fates. Their lives wander along different disparate [distinct] paths of the world's complex vagaries. They grow up as distinctive and undoubted individuals, yet they stand forth as far better clones than Dolly and her mother. Why have we overlooked this central principle in our fears about Dolly? Identical twins provide sturdy proof that inevitable differences of nurture guarantee the individuality and personhood of each human clone. . . . Why ask if Dolly has a soul or an independent life when we have never doubted the personhood or individuality of far more similar identical twins?[59]

Some cloning opponents are unconvinced by Gould's argument. Even if identical twins are more alike than a clone and its donor, they say, clones would lack the

Some of those who oppose cloning humans suggest that cloned individuals would lack the feeling of newness and uniqueness possessed by naturally born infants.

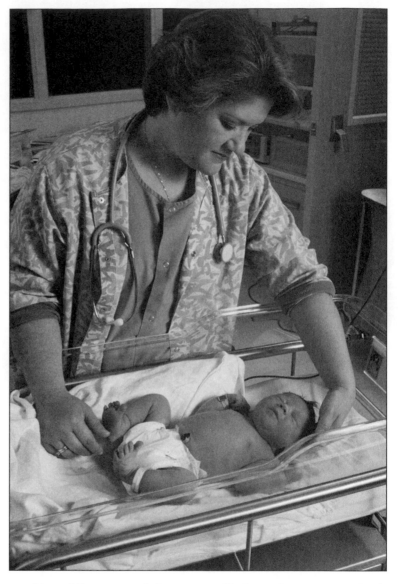

quality of "newness" that naturally born humans, including twins, possess. "There is no strong analogy between human cloning and natural identical twinning," declares bioethicist Stephen J. Post, "for in the latter case there is still the blessing of newness in the newborns, though they be two or more. While identical twins do occur naturally and are unique persons, this does not justify the temptation to impose external sameness more widely."[60]

Confusing Family Relationships

Post, along with many other concerned individuals, also fears that widespread human cloning might harm society in various ways. One major detrimental social effect, cloning opponents warn, will be a blurring or confusion of traditional roles and relationships within the family. According to Karen H. Rosenberg, director of the Law and Health Care Program at the University of Maryland School of Law:

> Adult cell cloning upsets our notion of familial relationships. Creation of a child by cloning requires the contribution of DNA material, an unfertilized egg and a ready womb. What language will we use to describe this "family?" By what criteria will we determine the claim of parental status of each of the contributors to the cloning process? [61]

Cloning proponent Lee Silver agrees that human cloning will change the dynamics of families and make some relationships more varied and complex. But he doubts this will be necessarily harmful, or even novel, pointing out that a good deal of variety and complexity already exist in many families. In addition to traditional biological fathers and mothers, he says, there are social fathers and mothers (those that raise children who are not their own for varying reasons), gestational (or surrogate) mothers (women who carry fetuses to term for women who are infertile), adoptive parents, single parents, and so forth. "As we think about all the variations on motherhood and fatherhood," Silver writes,

> it is clear that these concepts are not as easily defined as they once were when human reproduction was a mysterious process hidden from the view of all, within the womb of a woman. . . . Today, there is not one but many paths that can be followed to reach the goal of having [and/or raising] a child. The validity of any of these paths should be judged not by where or how development began, but by the love that a parent gives to the child after she or he is born. [62]

Nevertheless, say some concerned members of the debate, human cloning may introduce some strange new twists into the family unit that might create some confusing and perhaps regrettable and decidedly unethical situations. Margaret Talbot offers the following example:

> If a woman cloned herself and reared a child, she would be her own daughter's identical twin. If she had a husband, he would eventually find himself with a daughter who uncannily resembled his wife. Would this lead to confusion, even incest?[63]

In 1997, Pope John Paul II condemned human cloning as an attempt to imitate God.

Tampering in God's Domain?

Not surprisingly, the ethical and moral arguments against cloning also often have a religious dimension.

The President's Commission Weighs In

Soon after the announcement in 1997 of Dolly's birth, President Bill Clinton requested the group that advises the White House on ethical issues, the National Bioethics Advisory Commission, to consider the issue of human cloning. In June of that same year, the commission released its report (excerpted below), which concluded that, at least for the present, human cloning should be considered immoral.

The commission concludes that at this time it is morally unacceptable for anyone in the public or private sector, whether in a research or clinical setting, to attempt to create a child using somatic cell nuclear transfer cloning. We have reached a consensus on this point because current scientific information indicates that this technique is not safe to use in humans at this time. Indeed, we believe it would violate important ethical obligations were clinicians or researchers to attempt to create a child using these particular technologies, which are likely to involve unacceptable risks to the fetus and/or potential child. Moreover, in addition to safety concerns, many other serious ethical concerns have been identified [including possible harm to a clone's sense of individuality, potential damage to the institution of the family, and religious objections], which require much more widespread and careful public deliberation before this technology may be used.

There is a perception among many devout members of most major religions that making human beings by cloning, an artificial process, will amount to tampering in "God's domain." Shortly after the announcement in 1997 of Dolly's birth, Pope John Paul II condemned the concept of human cloning, calling it a tragic attempt by humans to imitate God's unique and special life-giving powers. Though the pope spoke on behalf of Catholics, many Protestants, Muslims, and Jews agree with his moral stance on human cloning. In March 1997 just after the announcement about Dolly, for example, *Time* magazine polled a random sample of Americans; when asked if cloning people is against the will of God, 74 percent answered yes. A 1997 report by the National Bioethics Advisory Commission (a group that advises the U.S. president on the ethical uses of science) summarized the main religious moral arguments against human cloning:

> Human beings should not probe the fundamental secrets or mysteries of life, which belong to God. Human beings lack the [divine] authority to make certain decisions about the beginning or ending of life. . . . Human beings are fallible [whereas God is infallible]. . . . Human beings do not have the knowledge . . . [or] the power to control the outcomes of actions or processes that is the mark of divine omnipotence [God's almighty power].[64]

Humans Play God for a Living?

This statement by Rudy Baum, managing editor of Chemical Engineering News, *from a 1997 article for that journal, makes the point that arguments about the morality of human cloning may have come too late to make any significant difference. "That moral Rubicon [point of no return] has already been crossed," he argues.*

Is that a moral catastrophe for humans? No. Is it the mark of our ultimate hubris [arrogance], our need to "play God"? Certainly. Playing God is what humans do for a living. We've been doing it for centuries. We rearranged the natural landscape through plant and animal breeding. We discovered vaccination and antibiotics to defeat plagues that once decimated populations. We exterminated species because they were in our way. We created reproductive technologies to aid people who would otherwise not be able to have children. . . . Now we've learned how to clone animals and, probably, people. It's all part of a continuum [ongoing series of related events], a technological imperative that is as unstoppable as the passage of time. Humans playing God isn't always pretty . . . but moral outrage at this juncture strikes me as disingenuous [avoiding or concealing the obvious truth] given the history of human meddling in the biosphere.

Responding to these powerful arguments, those who support research into human cloning point out that not all members of all religions are against such research. And just as different faiths have varying views about God's image and intent, many people have different views of where humanity's domain ends and God's domain begins. Moreover, the argument goes, in a society like that of the United States, which has laws protecting religious freedom (including freedom *from* religion as well as freedom *of* religion), no single religious group or view should be forced on everyone. Therefore, it is perfectly acceptable for individuals or groups to speak out against human cloning and refuse to avail themselves of its technology; but it is unacceptable for these individuals and groups to stop others from developing and using it. Not developing and using it, according to this view, could end up hurting society by denying it the potential benefits of human cloning. A statement by the International Academy of Humanism (an Amherst, New York–based group that supports free inquiry in all fields of human endeavor) puts it this way:

> The immediate question raised by the current debate over cloning is . . . do advocates of supernatural or spiritual agendas have truly meaningful qualifications to contribute to that debate? Surely everyone has the right to be heard. But we believe there is a very real danger that research with enormous potential benefits may be suppressed solely because it conflicts with some people's religious beliefs. It is important to recognize that similar religious objections were once raised against autopsies, anesthesia, artificial insemination, and the entire genetic revolution of our day—yet enormous benefits have accrued from each of these developments. A view of human nature rooted in humanity's mythical past ought not to be our primary criterion for making moral decisions about cloning.[65]

Two Views of the Future

These and other similar arguments for and against the development of human cloning will surely continue for a long time to come. Though the arguments are many, diverse, and often complex, perhaps their essences can be distilled down to two simplified opposing beliefs or positions about the future of human cloning. The first, held by the most emphatic opponents, is basically that both the concept and technology are potentially harmful and should be completely avoided, at least for the foreseeable future. In Leon Kass's view:

> The stakes are very high.... I exaggerate, but in the direction of the truth, when I insist that we are faced with having to decide nothing less than whether human procreation is going to remain human, whether children are going to be made rather than begotten, whether it is a good thing, humanly speaking, to say yes in principle to the road that leads (at best) to ... [dehumanization].... This is not business as usual, to be fretted about for a while but finally to be given our seal of approval. We must rise to the occasion and make our judgments as if the future of our humanity hangs in the balance. For so it does.[66]

At the opposite extreme in the debate, a good many scientists and others say that human cloning not only *should* proceed, but inevitably *will* proceed, no matter how much some people oppose it. "Attempts to limit this technology will be doomed to failure," says Silver.

> Many Tay-Sachs-carrying patients [those with a serious hereditary disease that human cloning shows promise of preventing] will surely feel that it is their "God-given" right to have access to a technology that allowed earlier couples to have non-afflicted children, and just as surely, there will always be a clinic or country that will accommodate their wishes. And if the technology is available for this one purpose, it will also be available for others.[67]

Those who disagree with Silver counter that attempts to limit human cloning *will* be initiated. The instrument of that limitation, they warn, will be laws banning or tightly regulating it. And indeed, in various parts of the world, such laws have already gone into effect. Whether or not such laws become standard across the globe or disappear over time as (and of course *if*) the technology proves beneficial, remains to be seen.

EPILOGUE

Should and Will Human Cloning Be Banned?

When the report of the National Bioethics Advisory Commission (which President Bill Clinton had asked to study human cloning) came out in 1997, it concluded that human cloning should be viewed, at least for the time being, as immoral. But the commission went further. It also recommended that laws be enacted restricting, regulating, or banning the technology. "Federal legislation should be enacted," the report stated, "to prohibit anyone from attempting, whether in a research or clinical setting, to create a child through somatic cell nuclear transfer cloning."[68]

This recommendation underscored the fears and worries held by many members of the U.S. Congress about the potential dangers of human cloning. They certainly reflected the same fears and worries voiced by many politicians, ethicists, and ordinary citizens, many of them calling for legal prohibitions against the new technology. "We should do all we can to prevent the cloning of human beings," said influential ethicist Leon Kass.

102

We should do this by means of an international legal ban if possible, and by a unilateral national ban [i.e., a ban by the U.S. government], at a minimum. Scientists may secretly undertake to violate such a law, but they will be deterred by not being able to stand up proudly to claim the credit for their technological bravado and success. Such a ban . . . will reassure the public that scientists are happy to proceed without violating the deep ethical norms and intuitions of the human community.[69]

Some other ethicists, as well as many scientists and other concerned citizens, understand that such fears are normal and often accompany the introduction of new and powerful technologies. But they feel that enacting laws against cloning is an overreaction that may impede scientific progress. "What's worrisome," says another influential ethicist, Arthur Caplan,

After the news of Dolly's birth appeared in 1997, then-U.S. president Bill Clinton asked the National Bioethics Advisory Commission to study human cloning.

is that [mainly out of fear of the unknown] people are going to say "We can't control anything here; let's turn back from the genetic revolution; let's ban it; let's stop funding it; the thing is dangerous. Cults have it, nuts have it [a reference to the human cloning efforts of the Raëlians, the Canadian UFO group]; who knows where this is going?"[70]

Overreaction or not, many governments across the globe have moved toward banning, or at least tightly regulating, human cloning research. In the wake of the announcement in 1997 of Dolly's creation, several countries banned all human cloning research, among them the United Kingdom, Denmark, Australia, Germany, and Japan. A few U.S. states, including California and Michigan, did the same. However, the U.S. government stopped short of a countrywide ban at that time. Instead, President Clinton opted for restricting the use of federal money to support human cloning research, issuing an executive order to that effect in March 1997. Then, in its report in June, the National Bioethics Advisory Commission upheld this move and also called on privately funded groups and labs to observe a voluntary moratorium [period of delay or inactivity] on such research.

Congressional Hearings on Cloning

In addition, the commission urged that members of the U.S. Congress hold hearings to consider human cloning regulations or bans. The hearings were held that same year. Experts on both sides of the issue expressed their opinions, including scientists who explained that human cloning research could go in one or both of two different directions. Cloning could possibly be used to reproduce human beings, they admitted; but "therapeutic" human cloning experiments would aim not to produce human fetuses but to fight genetic and other diseases. A general ban on cloning, they said, could halt promising research into cures for hemophilia, Tay-Sachs, and numerous other dreaded ailments.

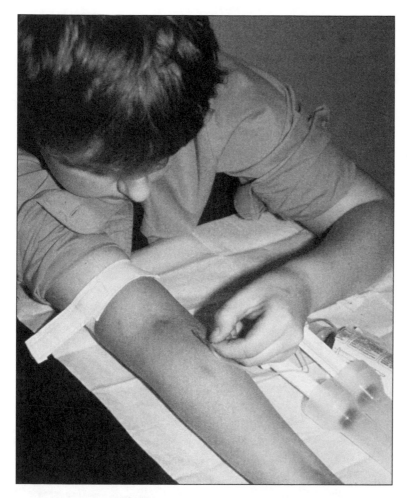

A hemophiliac gives himself a transfusion. Many scientists say that banning human cloning would unduly restrict research into possible cures for hemophilia and other genetic diseases.

Swayed by these arguments, the committee holding the hearings was reluctant to recommend an outright ban on all human cloning research. Instead, it ended up endorsing the recommendations already made by the commission, which also made a distinction between the two directions the research might take. Any laws the country might make against human cloning, the commission said,

> should be carefully written so as not to interfere with other important areas of scientific research. In particular, no new regulations are required regarding the cloning of human DNA sequences and cell lines, since neither activity raises the scientific and ethical issues that arise from the attempt

to create children through [cloning], and these fields of research have already provided important scientific and biomedical advances.[71]

The commission also called for Congress to "review the issue after a specified time period (three to five years) in order to decide whether the prohibition continues to be needed."[72] That review occurred on March 29, 2001, in a lively five-hour meeting of a House of Representatives subcommittee. Various scientists and other experts testified, including Brigitte Boisselier, head of the Raëlian human cloning program. As in 1997 the committee did not take an immediate clear-cut stand for or against the technology. Some legislators on the committee were disturbed to hear about the ongoing human cloning programs overseen by Boisselier and Panos Zavos and vowed that they would introduce a bill to ban all research in the area. But other members, repeating the concerns voiced by several scientists who testified, said they were reluctant to support such legislation. They pointed out that it would be extremely dif-

Dr. Panos Zavos (left) and Dr. Brigitte Boisellier (right) testify before a U.S. House of Representatives subcommittee.

ficult to word such a law so that it did not interfere with legitimate research, including that related to so-called therapeutic human cloning. Also, they said, any ban on human cloning might tread on the rights of American citizens to reproduce in any manner they see fit.

An Uncertain Future

For the moment, therefore, the legality of human cloning varies from one country or state to another. Regulations are few and inconsistent, and the likelihood and nature of any future bans or regulations remains uncertain. At present, no one knows whether a ban on human cloning will ever be passed by the U.S. Congress, or whether bans already in place in other countries will stand or fall. Opinions on both sides of the issue remain strong and more controversy surely lies ahead. However, a well-reasoned middle ground on the issue is bound to emerge eventually. Nearly everyone agrees that, even if the technology could be and was banned everywhere, some scientists would eventually proceed with it in secret. The fact is that human cloning almost certainly will happen. In that case, say many experts, any outright prohibition may realistically have to give way to careful regulation. Ruth Macklin, a professor of bioethics at the Albert Einstein College of Medicine in New York City, perhaps foreshadows this ultimate compromise on the contentious human cloning issue, saying:

Pampered, healthy, happy, and still periodically in the international spotlight, Dolly remains blissfully unaware of the scientific and social revolution set in motion by her birth.

> Even if human cloning offers no obvious benefits to humanity, why ban it? In a democratic society, we don't usually pass laws outlawing something before there is actual or probable evidence of harm. A moratorium on further research into human cloning might make sense, in

order to consider calmly the grave questions it raises. If the moratorium is then lifted, human cloning should remain a research activity for an extended period. And if it is ever attempted, it should—and no doubt will—take place only with careful scrutiny and layers of legal oversight. Most important, human cloning should be governed by the same laws that now protect human rights. A world not safe for cloned humans would be a world not safe for the rest of us. [73]

NOTES

Introduction: Cloning: An Increasingly Divisive Issue

1. Martha C. Nussbaum and Cass R. Sunstein, Introduction to Nussbaum and Sunstein, eds., *Clones and Clones: Facts and Fantasies About Human Cloning*. New York: W. W. Norton, 1998, p. 11.
2. David Jefferis, *Cloning: Frontiers of Genetic Engineering*. New York: Crabtree, 1999, p. 4.
3. Quoted in Margaret Talbot, "A Desire to Duplicate," *New York Times Magazine*, February 4, 2001, p. 40.
4. Quoted in Gina Kolata, *Clone: The Road to Dolly and the Path Ahead*. New York: William Morrow, 1998, p. 1.
5. Charles A. White, "The Controversy over Cloning May Be More Furious than the Abortion Debate," in M. L. Rantala and Arthur J. Milgram, eds., *Cloning: For and Against*. Chicago: Open Court, 1999, p. 76.

Chapter 1—Before Dolly: Cloning in Nature, Agriculture, and the Imagination

6. Daniel Cohen, *Cloning*. Brookfield, CT: Millbrook Press, 1998, p. 11.
7. Keay Davidson, "Vulnerable Farm Species," *Washington Times*, March 9, 1997, p. 3.
8. Quoted in Kolata, *Clone*, p. 61.
9. Lee M. Silver, *Remaking Eden: Cloning and Beyond in a Brave New World*. New York: Avon Books, 1997, p. 96.
10. Alvin Toffler, *Future Shock*. New York: Random House, 1970, p. 197.

11. Quoted in Kolata, *Clone*, p. 102.
12. Kolata, *Clone*, p. 95.

Chapter 2—A Big Splash for a Little Lamb: The Creation of Dolly

13. Cohen, *Cloning*, p. 30.
14. Kolata, *Clone*, p. 24.
15. Kolata, *Clone*, pp. 25–26.
16. Michael Specter and Gina Kolata, "After Decades and Many Missteps, Cloning Success," *New York Times*, March 3, 1997, p. 2.
17. Ian Wilmut et al., *The Second Creation: Dolly and the Age of Biological Control*. New York: Farrar, Straus, and Giroux, 2000, p. 213.
18. Wilmut et al., *Second Creation*, pp. 213, 216, 219.
19. Wilmut et al., *Second Creation*, pp. 209–10.
20. Wilmut et al., *Second Creation*, p. 219.
21. Quoted in Kolata, *Clone*, p. 37.

Chapter 3: Of Cows, Pigs, and Rats: Potential Medical Benefits of Animal Cloning

22. Wilmut et al., *Second Creation*, p. 33.
23. Quoted in Elizabeth Pennisi, "After Dolly, a Pharming Frenzy," *Science*, January 30, 1998, p. 3.
24. Pennisi, "After Dolly," p. 3.
25. Kolata, *Clone*, p. 9.
26. Kolata, *Clone*, p. 9.
27. Cohen, *Cloning*, pp. 105–106.
28. Jeanne DuPrau, *Cloning*. San Diego: Lucent Books, 2000, p. 32.

Chapter 4: Diversity and Dinosaur DNA: Cloning Endangered and Extinct Species

29. For an up-to-date general overview of what is presently known about this famous mass extinction, see Don Nardo, *The Extinction of the Dinosaurs*. San Diego: Lucent Books, 2002; one of the more comprehensive scholarly studies available is James L. Powell, *Night Comes to the Cretaceous: Comets, Craters,*

Controversy, and the Last Days of the Dinosaurs. New York: Harcourt Brace, 1998.

30. DuPrau, *Cloning,* pp. 36–37.
31. Quoted in Jon Cohen, "Can Cloning Help Save Beleaguered Species?" *Science,* May 30, 1997, p. 42.
32. Quoted in Jon Cohen, "Can Cloning Help Save Beleaguered Species?" p. 43.
33. Jon Cohen, "Can Cloning Help Save Beleaguered Species?" p. 43.
34. Jon Cohen, "Can Cloning Help Save Beleaguered Species?" p. 44.
35. Daniel Cohen, *Cloning,* p. 106.
36. Rob DeSalle and David Lindley, *The Science of Jurassic Park and the Lost World, or How to Build a Dinosaur.* New York: BasicBooks, 1997, pp. xxix, 9.
37. DeSalle and Lindley, *The Science of Jurassic Park and the Lost World,* p. 68.
38. Richard Stone, "Cloning the Woolly Mammoth," *Discover,* April 1999, p. 32.

Chapter 5: The Advent of Human Cloning: Who Will Be Cloned and Why?

39. Eric A. Posner and Richard A. Posner, "The Demand for Human Cloning," in Nussbaum and Sunstein, *Clones and Clones,* p. 233.
40. Talbot, "A Desire to Duplicate," p. 40.
41. Arthur Caplan, in a taped interview for "Sunday Morning," broadcast on March 11, 2001.
42. Talbot, "A Desire to Duplicate," p. 40.
43. Quoted in Talbot, "A Desire to Duplicate," p. 44.
44. Talbot, "A Desire to Duplicate," p. 43.
45. Talbot, "A Desire to Duplicate," p. 43.
46. Lee Silver, in a taped interview for "Sunday Morning," broadcast on March 11, 2001.
47. Quoted in Talbot, "A Desire to Duplicate," p. 67.
48. Talbot, "A Desire to Duplicate," p. 67.
49. Silver, "Sunday Morning," March 11, 2001.
50. Silver, *Remaking Eden,* pp. 150–51.

51. Silver, *Remaking Eden*, p. 109.
52. Quoted in Talbot, "A Desire to Duplicate," p. 68.

Chapter 6: Playing God?: Ethical and Moral Concerns About Human Cloning

53. Quoted in Talbot, "A Desire to Duplicate," p. 45.
54. Quoted in Gina Kolata, "Researchers Find Big Risk of Defect in Cloning Animals," *New York Times*, March 25, 2001, p. 12.
55. Gregory E. Pence, ed., *Flesh of My Flesh: The Ethics of Cloning*. New York: Rowman and Littlefield, 1998, p. 119.
56. Quoted in Pence, *Flesh of My Flesh*, p. 135.
57. Silver, *Remaking Eden*, p. 10.
58. Quoted in Gary E. McCuen, ed., *Cloning: Science and Society*. Hudson, WI: Gary E. McCuen, 1998, p. 58.
59. Stephen Jay Gould, "Dolly's Fashion and Louis's Passion," in Nussbaum and Sunstein, *Clones and Clones*, pp. 47–48.
60. Stephen J. Post, "Judeo-Christian Objections to Cloning," in Lisa Yount, ed., *Cloning*. San Diego: Greenhaven Press, 2000, p. 136.
61. Karen H. Rosenberg, "Adult Cell Cloning and Embryo Splitting: An Overview," in McCuen, *Cloning*, p. 36.
62. Silver, *Remaking Eden*, pp. 228–29.
63. Talbot, "A Desire to Duplicate," p. 45.
64. National Bioethics Advisory Commission, *Cloning Human Beings: Report and Recommendations*. Rockville, MD, 1997, pp. 45–46.
65. International Academy of Humanism, "Declaration in Defense of Cloning," *Free Inquiry*, Summer 1997, pp. 11–12.
66. Leon Kass, "The Wisdom of Repugnance," in Leon R. Kass and James Q. Wilson, *The Ethics of Human Cloning*. Washington, DC: AEI Press, 1998, pp. 12–13.
67. Silver, *Remaking Eden*, pp. 264–65.

Epilogue—Should and Will Human Cloning Be Banned?

68. National Bioethics Advisory Commission, *Cloning Human Beings*, p. 109.

69. Leon Kass, "Human Cloning Should Be Banned," in Paul A. Winters, ed., *Cloning*. San Diego: Greenhaven Press, 1998, pp. 45–46.

70. Caplan, "Sunday Morning," March 11, 2001.

71. National Bioethics Advisory Commission, *Cloning Human Beings*, p. 109.

72. National Bioethics Advisory Commission, *Cloning Human Beings*, p. 109.

73. Ruth Macklin, "Human Cloning? Don't Just Say No," *U.S. News &World Report*, March 10, 1997, p. 16.

For Further Reading

Daniel Cohen, *Cloning*. Brookfield, CT: Millbrook Press, 1998. A well-written, easy to understand, and interesting exploration of cloning and modern conceptions of it.

Jeanne DuPrau, *Cloning*. San Diego: Lucent Books, 2000. A well-organized, thorough, and informative overview of the cloning phenomenon, covering plant cloning, animal cloning, possible medical benefits of cloning, and the ethical and legal considerations of possible human cloning.

David Jefferis, *Cloning: Frontiers of Genetic Engineering*. New York: Crabtree, 1999. Beautifully illustrated with color photos and drawings, this is an excellent introduction for young people to cloning and related topics, such as genes, cells, and DNA.

Linda J. Singleton, *Regeneration*. New York: Berkley Publishing Group, 2000. Aimed at young readers, this and the following sequels by the same author are well-written and thought-provoking fiction works dealing with cloning. The overall premise is that a group of teenagers discover that they are clones who have certain special powers that allow them to fight evil.

——, *The Search*. New York: Berkley Publishing Group, 2000.

——, *The Truth*. New York: Berkley Publishing Group, 2000.

——, *The Imposter*. New York: Berkley Publishing Group, 2000.

——, *The Killer*. New York: Berkley Publishing Group, 2001.

MAJOR WORKS CONSULTED

Lori B. Andrews, *The Clone Age: Adventures in the New World of Reproductive Technology*. New York: Henry Holt, 1999. An excellent overview of the cloning phenomenon and related topics.

Michael Crichton, *Jurassic Park*. New York: Knopf, 1990. The famous novel that inspired the equally famous film about scientists who succeed in cloning dinosaurs from genetic material found in the digestive tracts of ancient insects preserved in amber. Though fiction, it raises and explores questions about the cloning of extinct animal species that scientists are actually beginning to address.

Rob DeSalle and David Lindley, *The Science of Jurassic Park and the Lost World, or How to Build a Dinosaur*. New York: BasicBooks, 1997. A brilliant and fascinating look at the scientific technology and possibilities involved in the cloning of extinct animal species. Highly recommended.

Leon R. Kass and James Q. Wilson, *The Ethics of Human Cloning*. Washington, DC: AEI Press, 1998. A thoughtful, well-informed view of some of the ethical and moral concerns surrounding cloning, including how such cloning technology and its products might affect the family.

Gina Kolata, *Clone: The Road to Dolly and the Path Ahead*. New York: William Morrow, 1998. Kolata, a noted science writer for the *New York Times*, delivers an informative, thought-provoking summary of the various scientific discoveries, attitudes, and debates related to cloning before Dolly the sheep became the first animal clone in 1996.

Paul Lauritzen, *Cloning and the Future of Human Embryo Research*. New York: Oxford University Press, 2001. A well-balanced summary of present knowledge about cloning humans and the real possibility that such technology will soon be used to create human clones.

Ira Levin, *The Boys from Brazil*. New York: Random House, 1976. The suspenseful novel that inspired the 1978 film starring Laurence Olivier and Gregory Peck. In this story about how the evil Nazi doctor, Josef Mengele, attempts to clone the infamous Adolf Hitler, Levin exploits some of the worst fears about the possible uses of cloning; however, he tempers it by addressing the reality that clones would not be exact duplicates of the cloned individual, even if they were brought up in environments similar to that of the original person. Both the book and movie are a must for anyone interested in the subject of cloning.

Barbara MacKinnon, ed., *Human Cloning: Science, Ethics, and Public Policy*. Champaign: University of Illinois Press, 2000. A well-chosen and very informative series of essays dealing with various aspects of the cloning issue, including the morality of human cloning and whether or not human cloning should be regulated or banned.

Martha C. Nussbaum and Cass R. Sunstein, eds., *Clones and Clones: Facts and Fantasies About Human Cloning*. New York: W. W. Norton, 1998. Parts of the book consist of discussions of the known facts about cloning, others that attempt to dispel some of the common popular fallacies about cloning, such as the idea that a person's clone will have his or her same mental faculties or even the same memories. There are also essays questioning the ethics of cloning.

M. L. Rantala and Arthur J. Milgram, eds., *Cloning: For and Against*. Chicago: Open Court, 1999. This excellent collection of essays about the cloning debate addresses such issues as the possible medical and societal benefits of cloning, whether a clone has a soul, whether cloning should be banned or at least regulated, and so forth. Highly recommended.

Lee M. Silver, *Remaking Eden: Cloning and Beyond in a Brave New World*. New York: Avon Books, 1997. One of the better recent books about cloning, this one covers, among other topics, in vitro fertilization; how cloning went from being science fiction to science fact; the complex paternal and maternal questions raised by cloning; the possibility that, given the advent of human cloning, people will want to design their children to certain specifications; and so on.

Margaret Talbot, "A Desire to Duplicate," *New York Times Magazine*, February 4, 2001. A long, well-written informative tract summarizing the state of the art of human cloning and identifying the scientists and labs in the process of working toward this goal in the early months of 2001.

Jon Turney, *Frankenstein's Footsteps: Science, Genetics, and Popular Culture*. New Haven: Yale University Press, 1998. A brisk exploration of changing public attitudes about cloning and the way the public often fears or sees a distorted image of science and its newer, more controversial creations.

Ian Wilmut et al., "Viable Offspring Derived from Fetal and Adult Mammalian Cells," *Nature*, February 27, 1997. The seminal article announcing the creation of Dolly the sheep, the first mammal cloned from an adult cell.

Ian Wilmut et al., *The Second Creation: Dolly and the Age of Biological Control*. New York: Farrar, Straus, and Giroux, 2000. The researchers who cloned Dolly in 1996 explain their initial goals, their experiments, how they made Dolly, their conclusions, and the possible implications of their work. An important document in the cloning literature.

Lisa Yount, ed., *Cloning*. San Diego: Greenhaven Press, 2000. A very well chosen series of essays about cloning, covering the cloning of Dolly and its importance, cloning endangered species, movies and other media presentations of cloning, legal implications of cloning, ethical concerns, and much more. Highly recommended.

ADDITIONAL WORKS CONSULTED

Books

Peter Aldhous, "The Fears of a Clone," *New Scientist*, February 21, 1998.

Gary B. Anderson and George E. Seidel, "Cloning for Profit," *Science*, May 29, 1998.

Sharon Begely, "Little Lamb, Who Made Thee?" *Newsweek*, March 10, 1997.

——, "Spring Cloning," *Newsweek*, June 30, 1997.

Jon Cohen, "Can Cloning Help Save Beleaguered Species?" *Science*, May 30, 1997.

Keay Davidson, "Vulnerable Farm Species," *Washington Times*, March 9, 1997.

Karl Drlica, *Understanding DNA and Gene Cloning: A Guide for the Curious*. New York: John Wiley, 1992.

John S. Feinberg and Paul D. Feinberg, *Ethics for a Brave New World*. Wheaton, IL: Crossway Books, 1993.

Willard Gaylin, "The Frankenstein Myth Becomes a Reality: We Have the Awful Knowledge to Make Exact Copies of Human Beings," *New York Times Magazine*, March 5, 1972.

Meg Gordon, "Suffering of the Lambs," *New Scientist*, April 26, 1997.

Christine Gorman, "To Ban or Not to Ban?" *Time*, June 16, 1997.

J.B. Gurdon and Alan Colman, "The Future of Cloning," *Nature*, December 16, 1999.

Charles C. Harbin, *Cloning, Gene Expression, and Protein Purification: Experimental Procedures and Process Rationale*. New York: Oxford University Press, 2001.

Wray Herbert et al., "The World After Cloning," *U.S. News &World Report*, March 10, 1997.

Aldous Huxley, *Brave New World*. New York: Harper and Row, 1946.

International Academy of Humanism, "Declaration in Defense of Cloning," *Free Inquiry*, Summer 1997.

Jeffrey Kluger, "Will We Follow the Sheep?" *Time*, March 10, 1997.

Gina Kolata, "Researchers Find Big Risk of Defect in Cloning Animals," *New York Times*, March 25, 2001.

Ruth Macklin, "Human Cloning? Don't Just Say No," *U.S. News &World Report*, March 10, 1997.

Jay Maeder, "Bring 'em Back Alive," *U.S. News &World Report*, October 13, 1997.

Charles C. Mann and Mark L. Plummer, *Noah's Choice: The Future of Endangered Species*. New York: Knopf, 1995.

Michael Mautner, "Will Cloning End Human Evolution?" *Futurist*, November/December 1997.

Gary E. McCuen, ed., *Cloning: Science and Society*. Hudson, WI: Gary E. McCuen, 1998.

Lynn Messina, ed., *Biotechnology*. New York: H. W. Wilson, 2000.

National Bioethics Advisory Commission, *Cloning Human Beings: Report and Recommendations*. Rockville, MD: 1997.

Charles Pellegrino, "Resurrecting Dinosaurs," *Omni*, Fall 1995.

Gregory E. Pence, ed., *Flesh of My Flesh: The Ethics of Cloning*. New York: Rowman and Littlefield, 1998.

Elizabeth Pennisi, "After Dolly, a Pharming Frenzy," *Science*, January 30, 1998; and "Cloned Mice Provide Company for Dolly," *Science*, July 24, 1998.

David Rorvik, *In His Image: The Cloning of a Man*. Philadelphia: Lippincott, 1978.

Julian Savulescu, "Should We Clone Human Beings? Cloning as a Source of Tissue for Transplantation," *Journal of Medical Ethics*, April 1999.

Michael Specter and Gina Kolata, "A New Creation: The Path to Cloning," *New York Times*, March 3, 1997; and "After Decades and Many Missteps, Cloning Success," *New York Times*, March 3, 1997.

Gregory Stock, ed., *Engineering the Human Germline: An Exploration of the Science and Ethics of Altering the Genes We Pass to Our Children*. New York: Oxford University Press, 2000.

Richard Stone, "Cloning the Woolly Mammoth," *Discover*, April 1999.

Alan Taylor, "Silence of the Lamb," *New Yorker*, March 17, 1997.

Alvin Toffler, *Future Shock*. New York: Random House, 1970.

John Travis, "A Fantastical Experiment," *Science News*, April 5, 1997.

Gretchen Vogel, "Company Gets Rights to Cloned Human Embryos," *Science*, January 28, 2000.

Ian Wilmut, "Dolly's False Legacy," *Time*, January 11, 1999.

Edward O. Wilson, *The Diversity of Life*. Cambridge, MA: Harvard University Press, 1992.

Paul A. Winters, ed., *Cloning*. San Diego: Greenhaven Press, 1998.

Television Documentaries on Cloning

20/20, February 16, 2001.

60 Minutes, March 11, 2001.

Sunday Morning, March 11, 2001.

INDEX

PICTURE CREDITS

About the Author

In addition to his acclaimed volumes on ancient civilizations, historian Don Nardo has published several books for young people examining important modern scientific discoveries and topics, among them *The Origin of Species: Darwin's Theory of Evolution, Germs: Mysterious Microorganisms,* and *The Extinction of the Dinosaurs.* Mr. Nardo lives with his wife Christine in Massachusetts.

DATE DUE